100 GREAT
OLYMPIC MOMENTS

by Jon Allison

PARACHUTE
PRESS, INC.

Parachute Press, Inc.
156 Fifth Avenue
New York, New York 10010

First printing: January 1992
Printed in the U.S.A.

Design by Michel Design

COVER PHOTO CREDITS:
Jackie Joyner-Kersee © All Sport Photography
Carl Lewis © All Sport Photography
Steffi Graff © All Sport Photography
1980 U.S. Hockey Team © David Drapkin
Crowd shot © David Drapkin

All the information in this book is up-to-date as of 1991,
before the 1992 Olympics in Albertville and Barcelona.

CONTENTS

INTRODUCTION

The Olympic Games can grip the attention and imagination of the entire world. Every four years thousands of athletes from all different countries compete in this unique sporting event. The Olympic athletes are the best of the best. And together they strive to break the unbreakable records—to be the fastest, the strongest—and to push themselves to seemingly impossible limits.

The Olympic Games actually started in ancient Greece almost 3,000 years ago. Every four years, the greatest athletes in Greece gathered at Olympia and competed in chariot races, horse races, running, throwing, boxing, and wrestling. For the days of the Olympics, politics was forgotten. Those early Olympics were not like the Games of today. The athletes themselves had to show up early to prepare the facilities for their competition (imagine if that were done today!). And when the 40,000 or so spectators appeared for the Games, they had to endure a little discomfort too: there were no seats in the stadium!

Centuries later it was those ancient Greek Games that inspired Baron Pierre de Coubertin of France to propose the first modern Olympic Games. The baron was interested in fitness, and he saw the Olympics as a way of getting more people involved in exercise and sports. He also believed that the Games could provide wholesome competition between countries and promote world peace. By 1896, the baron succeeded in getting several nations to participate in the first modern Olympics in Athens. The Greeks felt they deserved the honor of hosting these Games—and they got it.

And so the Games began. Even though boycotts have sometimes cut down the number of participating countries and two world wars have temporarily stopped the Olympics altogether, Baron de Coubertin's dream-come-true will celebrate its 100th anniversary in 1996 in Atlanta, Georgia, U.S.A.

100 Great Olympic Moments come to life again in these pages. Some of the moments are joyful, others are sad. You will read about awesome athletic feats, weird moments, tragic times. You will meet people you won't be able to forget, athletes who overcame almost impossible odds to win Olympic gold. All this and more is what makes the Olympic Games so special.

CHAPTER ONE
SUPER FEATS

Athletes pushing themselves beyond limits, striving for almost impossible goals and achieving victory—that's what some of the greatest Olympic moments are all about!

Summer Games/Track and Field

The Legend of Bright Path

JIM THORPE—1912—WON GOLD MEDALS IN BOTH PENTATHLON AND DECATHLON

The best male athlete of all time? More than one expert would vote for Jim Thorpe. A full-blooded Native American (his mother was a Potawatomi and his father a Sac and Fox), Thorpe was called Bright Path by his Indian brothers. He excelled in every sport he tried, and Thorpe stood the sporting world on its ear during the 1912 Games in Stockholm, Sweden.

When he was fifteen, Jim was sent from his Oklahoma birthplace to the Carlisle (Pennsylvania) Indian School. The Carlisle football team, coached by the legendary Pop Warner and starring the unmatched Thorpe, beat most of the nation's famous college football powers. Then when Thorpe tried track and baseball, he found he was just as good in those sports too. In fact, for a couple of summers, he played semipro baseball for $60 a month in expense money.

When the 1912 Olympics rolled around, Thorpe was a shoo-in for the U.S. team. The only question was: which events would he take part in? Jim did it the hard way, selecting the pentathlon (five events) and the decathlon (ten events). It was the most grueling program ever undertaken by one athlete in a single Olympics.

In the pentathlon, Thorpe finished first in the long jump, 200-meter dash, discus throw, and 1,500-meter run. He was third in the javelin, but he easily captured the gold.

The decathlon was even tougher, but Thorpe handled it with ease. He won four events outright and wound up winning the gold by an unheard-of nearly 700 points.

But his joy was short-lived. Early the next year (1913), Olympic officials found out about Thorpe's baseball days. They decided Thorpe was a professional athlete, stripped him of his medals, and struck his marks from the record book. Thorpe was heartbroken and fans were outraged. A steady stream of protests was ignored by the International Olympic Committee.

Thorpe continued in sports, playing six years of major-league baseball before turning to pro football in 1919. But perhaps his greatest moment came in 1983, thirty years after his death. That's when the International Olympic Committee finally agreed to restore Jim Thorpe's medals and records to the Olympic Hall of Fame.

Jesse Owens's Games

JESSE OWENS—1936—FOUR GOLD TRACK AND FIELD MEDALS

Nazi leader Adolf Hitler sat in his private box at the 1936 Olympics in Berlin, Germany, looking down at the competitors on the track. Hitler was sure his "master race"—white Germans—would lead the field, and he looked forward to their victory.

The crowd suddenly hushed as a lone black athlete named Jesse Owens approached the starting block for the 100-meter dash. All eyes, especially Hitler's, were on the slim American sprinter/jumper. The pressure was on.

Jesse exploded out of the block and sprinted ahead. With his graceful running style, standing practically straight up with little extra motion, he was easy to see, especially since he led the field. He won the race, his time of 10.3 seconds setting a new world and Olympic record. Unfortunately the record (not the victory) was disqualified because the wind at his back was a bit faster than the rules allowed.

Next came the long jump. Jesse had fouled (stepped over the starting line) on several attempts. With only one jump left, he trailed Germany's Luz Long. Adolf Hitler was already preparing to welcome Long to his box for a victory celebration. Taking care not to foul, Jesse took off at the back end of the board and floated through the air an Olympic record-breaking distance of 26 feet, 5 1/2 inches to win the event. It was the first Olympic jump over 26 feet. Hitler was furious—a black man was showing up his white German athletes.

And Jesse wasn't finished. On a cold, blustery day, he swept the 200 meters in 20.7 seconds, a full half-second faster than the world mark for 200 meters around a curve. Then he led off the U.S. 4 x 100-meter relay team. The American team finished first in 39.8 seconds, another world record.

Jesse's Olympic performance was nothing less than incredible: four gold medals, two world records, one Olympic record. But that's only part of the story. Jesse Owens didn't just defeat the athletes running on the track with him; he defeated the ugly idea that blacks are inferior to whites. Adolf Hitler had looked forward to a triumph at the Berlin Olympics, but Jesse Owens made certain that Hitler wound up with a major failure.

Summer Games/Track and Field

The Kid from Tulare

BOB MATHIAS—1948—SEVENTEEN-YEAR-OLD WINS DECATHLON GOLD

At age fourteen, in 1945, Olympic glory was the farthest thing from Bob Mathias's mind. He was skinny and weak, a victim of anemia, a condition in which the blood has too few red cells.

Treated by his doctor-father, Bob gradually recovered. He grew tall and strong. He became an athlete, perhaps the best that his hometown of Tulare, California, has ever seen. He starred in football, basketball, and track.

It was after a track meet that his high school coach suggested that Bob try out for the 1948 Olympic decathlon team. "Sure," said Bob, even though he'd never even *tried* four of the ten events that make up the decathlon.

Even for a mature, experienced athlete, the decathlon is a struggle. The ten events are crammed into only two days. The 100-meter dash, long jump, shot put, high jump, and 400-meter dash fill the first day. The 110-meter high hurdles, discus, pole vault, javelin throw, and 1,500-meter run are conducted on day two.

On August 5, 1948, on a dark and rainy day in London, England, seventeen-year-old Mathias started what would be the test of his life. The athletes were on the field from ten in the morning until eight at night. Though Bob didn't win a single event outright, he tied for first in the high jump (6 feet, 1 1/4 inches) and, miraculously, held third place in the standings.

The weather didn't change on August 6. In fact, it was worse. London was bathed in rain, fog, and mud. By the time the last event was run at 10:00 p.m., Mathias was in the lead. But then came the grueling 1,500-meter race. It was going to take everything he had and more. If only he could stay close in the long race, the gold would be his. He did. As he crossed the finish line in

11

first place, he flopped into his father's arms. "Never again," he gasped. "Never again."

Fortunately, he didn't mean it. In 1952, he was at the Olympics again, this time in Helsinki, Finland. And again he made history. He set a new world decathlon record. He also became the first man ever to win two straight Olympic decathlon championships, and he was the youngest winner of a men's track and field event in the history of the Olympics.

Czech Mate

EMIL ZATOPEK—1952—WON ALL THREE DISTANCE RACES

When Czechoslovakia's Emil Zatopek arrived in Helsinki, Finland, for the 1952 Olympics, everyone expected him to do well. But few expected him to accomplish the Games' all-time record distance triple—the 5,000-meter, the 10,000-meter, *and* the marathon.

He easily won the 10,000-meter title, setting an Olympic record (29:17.0). In the 5,000, he held off four challengers in the final strides, setting another Olympic mark (14:06.6). What more could he accomplish? The marathon.

"I've got to give it a try," said Zatopek, who had never run a marathon. Running the 26.2 miles wouldn't be a problem, but he didn't have a clue about race strategy. Emil knew that Jim

Peters of England was the favorite, and he decided to tag along with him. Mile after mile, Peters, Zatopek, and Sweden's Gustav Jansson ran stride for stride. Finally, at about the 20-mile mark, Peters suffered leg cramps and had to drop out. That's when Zatopek decided to pull away from Jansson. It was the perfect move.

In his first marathon ever, the Czech won his third gold of the Games. His time? Only the fastest marathon in Olympic history until then (2:23:03.2)!

Airborne Oerter

AL OERTER—1956-1968—WINS FOUR STRAIGHT GOLDS

It's certainly impressive to win a gold medal in the Olympics, but winning the gold in four *straight* Olympic Games is absolutely incredible—so incredible that only one person has ever done it!

American discus thrower Al Oerter, the twenty-year-old broad-shouldered superstar from West Babylon, New York, started his fabulous Olympic streak in 1956 at Melbourne, Australia. Surrounded by the world's greatest throwers, Oerter was not expected to do much, but the star uncorked an Olympic record throw of 184 feet, 11 inches and took home a surprising gold medal.

Still, Oerter was no better than a cofavorite when the world's best gathered in Rome, Italy, in 1960. Al's American teammate, Rink Babka, had beaten Oerter at the Olympic trials and, with one throw to go at the Olympics, held a slim lead over the defending champ. But Babka noticed a flaw in Al's delivery and pointed it out to him. Al took the advice, and his final throw of 194 feet, 2 inches set another Olympic mark and won him a second straight gold. And he still wasn't through.

Pain from a neck injury and Czech star Ludvik Danek stood between Oerter and his third gold in Tokyo, Japan, in '64. Again, Al waited for his final chance before making the Olympics' first 200-foot throw (beating the magic number by 1 inch). Gold medal number three was presented a few minutes later.

No one had ever won four straight Olympic gold medals. That was the challenge for Al Oerter in Mexico City, Mexico in '68. A rain delay bothered most of the other athletes, but not the veteran Oerter. He'd been there before. He was ready for anything. When he delivered another new record throw (212 feet, 6 inches, more than 5 feet farther than he'd ever thrown), the competition wilted. Four Olympics, four gold medals; Oerter had done the impossible.

Rafer's Comeback

RAFER JOHNSON—1960— DECATHLON GOLD

The winner of the Olympic decathlon is considered the world's greatest athlete. In Rome, Italy, in 1960, Rafer Johnson wanted that title for himself. He had come close four years before in Melbourne, Australia, when he won the silver medal. Now he wanted the gold.

His archrival, C. K. Yang of Taiwan, was Johnson's teammate at UCLA and one of his best friends. Yang was a world-class decathlete with a good shot at the gold medal. Johnson knew there was only one way he could win—he had to focus on Yang, stay on his tail, and never let up on him.

From the beginning, the decathlon was a two-man race as Yang and Johnson battled head-to-head. By the final event, the 1,500-meter run, Johnson had a narrow lead. To win the gold, Yang would have to beat Johnson by 10 seconds. Johnson knew that Yang could outrun him. Johnson was exhausted, but he had to put every ounce of energy into this race.

They made the final turn and headed for the finish line. Yang was ahead. Johnson speeded up. Yang did beat him—but only by 1.2 seconds.

The rivalry between Yang and Johnson may have helped them perform at their peak—they both broke the Olympic decathlon scoring record. Yang was the first Taiwanese ever to win an

Olympic medal. And Rafer Johnson finally had his gold.

The Perfect Jump

BOB BEAMON—1968—LONGEST-HELD LONG JUMP RECORD

Olympic records are often broken by just a split second in time or a fraction of an inch in distance. But in 1968 in Mexico City, Mexico, Bob Beamon achieved one of the greatest moments in sports of all time.

Beamon was a great American long jumper. He came to Mexico City determined to break the 28-foot mark and set a new world's record. But he almost blew it in the preliminary round.

Beamon had a tendency to foul on his jumps. In the three-jump preliminary round, he fouled on his first two jumps. One more foul and he'd be out of the meet. Teammate Ralph Boston counseled Bob. "Take it easy," he advised. "Try to take off a few inches behind the board." It worked. Beamon easily qualified on his third try.

In the finals, the first three jumpers fouled. Then it was Beamon's turn. Bob stood at the end of the runway for 20 seconds, gathering his thoughts. Then he sped down the strip, hitting the takeoff board perfectly. He rose into the air, sailing unusually high. He hit the pit so powerfully that he immediately sprang up and landed outside the sandy area.

It was easy to see that Beamon's jump had been a long one. The automatic measuring device, installed especially for the Games, couldn't measure the leap. A standard steel tapemeasure was needed. Up on the scoreboard, the numbers 8.90 meters flashed. Bob knew he had a record, but he didn't know exactly what it was until the meters were converted to feet and inches. When the announcement was made, the other competitors were shocked. His distance was 29 feet, 2 1/2 inches. He had beaten the record by 21 inches! Beamon himself felt faint. He suffered a seizure and fell to the ground in shock.

In just a few brief seconds in 1968, Bob Beamon changed the sport of long jumping forever. Even though his world record has now been broken, it lasted twenty-four years, through six Olympiads! Many experts say Beamon's jump was the single greatest individual effort in the world of sports.

Summer Games/Track and Field

Viren's Double Double

LASSE VIREN—1972 & 1976—FIRST TO WIN TWO STRAIGHT DISTANCE DOUBLES

Winning an Olympic distance race (5,000 or 10,000 meters) is a tremendous achievement. Winning both in a single Olympiad is incredible. Winning both in two straight Games? That super feat has been accomplished only once—by Finland's Lasse Viren.

The soft-spoken Finnish policeman, a strong and powerful runner, nearly had his 1972 Olympic dreams shattered in his first race. In the 10,000 meters in Munich, West Germany, Viren stumbled, then fell midway through the race. For most runners, that would be the end. Not for Viren. Lasse quickly jumped up and sprinted ahead. One lap later, he had moved into second place. Then with 600 meters to go, he blasted away from the pack to win. His time of 27:38.4 set a new world record.

Then Viren won the 5,000 meters, setting another new Olympic mark of 13:26.4.

But scandal tainted the Finn's performances. Lasse was accused of blood doping, a process that involves extracting blood in advance of a race. The blood is frozen, then thawed, and finally reinjected just before the race. As a result, the runner's blood can carry additional oxygen, which gives a runner more energy. The charge was never proven. Viren returned for the 1976 Games in Montreal, Canada, more determined than ever to prove that he was number one.

First, he beat Portugal's Carlos Sousa Lopes by nearly five seconds to take his second straight 10,000-meter title (27:40.38). Then, in the 5,000 meters, he outran New Zealand's Dick Quax to win in 13:24.76, breaking his own Olympic mark. No one had ever won two straight Olympic 5,000-meter titles and, of course, no one had ever won

two straight distance doubles (5,000 and 10,000)—
until Lasse Viren.

The Streaker

EDWIN MOSES—1976-1988— LONGEST WINNING STREAK IN THE 400-METER HURDLES

The 400-meter hurdles is track and field's "killer"
race. It's a long sprint interrupted by ten hurdles
to jump over. For nearly a decade, including two
Olympics, America's Edwin Moses "owned" the
race.

Moses discovered the 400-meter hurdles
during the spring of 1976, just four months before
the '76 Olympics in Montreal, Canada. He took
to the event as if he'd been running it all his life.
U.S. Olympic coach Leroy Walker took one look
at Moses and knew instantly that he had a
champion on his hands. "I told coaches all over
the world that their athletes were competing for
second place," said Walker. Moses was as good as
his coach's word. He took the gold in Montreal and
set a new world record (47.64 seconds).

A year later, in September 1977, Moses won
the World Cup title in Dusseldorf, West Germany, and began one of the most incredible winning streaks in sports history. He did not lose
another hurdles final for nine years.

Edwin's shot at a second straight Olympic

gold medal was dashed as a result of the American boycott of the 1980 Games in Moscow, U.S.S.R. Moses was bitterly disappointed, but he managed to keep his winning streak going right through the 1984 Games in Los Angeles, California. His time of 47.75 seconds produced an easy victory.

What was Moses's secret? The ability to take only thirteen steps between the hurdles. Most runners had to take fourteen or even fifteen. Though his streak finally ended at 107 straight wins in 1987, Moses remained king of the hurdlers until he finished third to American Andre Phillips and Senegal's Amadou Dia Ba at the 1988 Olympic Games in Seoul, South Korea. But even as the winner, Phillips, accepted congratulations from athletes, fans, and the media, he continued to tell anyone who would listen: "Edwin Moses is still the best!"

Summer Games/Track and Field

Going Four the Gold

CARL LEWIS—1984—MATCHED OWENS'S FOUR TRACK AND FIELD GOLDS

Carl Lewis began long jumping in his backyard almost as soon as he learned how to run. His inspiration was Jesse Owens; his goal, to match Owens's four Olympic medals.

Lewis's attempt to equal Owens began with

the 100-meter dash in Los Angeles, California, in 1984. No sweat. The twenty-three-year-old broke the magic 10-second barrier. His time of 9.99 seconds was the best ever run at low altitude, where the air is heavier and times "slower."

Next came the long jump. Carl had long talked about matching Bob Beamon's sixteen-year-old record of 29 feet, 2 1/2 inches. He didn't come close, but his first leap of 28 feet, 1/4 inch was easily good enough to win his second gold. Lewis took one more shot at the Beamon mark, then packed up for the day. The crowd, expecting the full allotment of six attempts, booed Lewis's apparent lack of effort. But Carl, knowing that the upcoming 200-meter dash and the 4 x 100 relay required at least seven more races, was pacing himself carefully.

Properly prepared, Lewis dug in for a tough 200-meter race. Quick out of the blocks, he held off the competition and set another Olympic record (19.80 seconds). Finally he followed Sam Graddy, Ron Brown, and Calvin Smith, whipping through the 4 x 100 relay in world record time (37.83 seconds). Carl had done it! He had his moment. He had matched his idol Jesse Owens by winning four gold medals.

Seven Ways Better

JACKIE JOYNER-KERSEE—1988—SET WORLD HEPTATHLON RECORD

In 1984, Jackie Joyner-Kersee lost the gold medal in the heptathlon by only 6/100ths of a second. She vowed that the gold would be hers in 1988.

Athletic success was nothing new in the Joyner family. Jackie's brother Al, an Olympic triple-jump champion in 1984, married Florence Griffith-Joyner, herself a champion athlete. Jackie's husband and coach, Bob Kersee, was a well-known track coach at UCLA. Now Jackie was ready to make her own mark in the heptathlon—a grueling seven-event contest.

In Seoul, South Korea, she got off to a great start, but her joy was short-lived. She twisted her knee in the high jump. It was painful and could collapse at any time, but she still had two more days of competition to go.

With her knee aching, she scored a personal best on the shot put and ran the 200-meter dash in 22.56 seconds. She set an Olympic record in the long jump and ran 800 meters in 2:08.51. She won the gold medal easily, beating her nearest rival by 397 points and setting a new world record—all with an injured knee. She celebrated by taking two days off and then coming back to win the gold medal in the long jump, setting another Olympic record.

King of the Heavyweights?

TEOFILO STEVENSON—1972-1980— FIRST TO WIN THREE HEAVYWEIGHT BOXING GOLDS

Montreal, Canada, 1976. Cuba's Teofilo Stevenson is in the ring, fighting Romania's Mircea Simon. But Simon has seen Stevenson fight. He's so terrified of him that, rather than try to fight him, he runs away!

Simon can't run forever. Stevenson catches up to him at last and delivers one big, powerful punch. Simon's corner immediately calls off the bout. Stevenson has won his second Olympic gold medal.

Boxing promoters descend on Stevenson, offering him millions of dollars to turn pro, but he refuses. "Turning pro would interfere with my studies," he says.

The promoters can't believe it. What kind of person would turn down a professional boxing career for his studies?

Some boxing fans say Teofilo Stevenson ranks as the greatest heavyweight fighter ever, over names like Joe Louis, Rocky Marciano, and Muhammad Ali. No one can say for sure, because he never fought professionally. But he *did* set an Olympic record—the first heavyweight to win two gold medals in a row—in 1972 and 1976—and then, even more incredibly, a third in 1980. Still, the question of where Stevenson would rank on the all-time heavyweight list will never be answered.

The Boxing Class

AMERICAN BOXING TEAM—1976— BEST EVER

For sheer power, speed, and courage, Olympic boxing has never seen anything like the 1976 American team. This team, composed of some of the U.S.'s best boxers ever, provided some of the greatest moments in Olympic ring history.

Start with Sugar Ray Leonard. The power hitter from Palmer Park, Maryland, captivated fans in the Montreal, Canada, arena and TV viewers at home with his flashy style and winning personality. In his Olympic light-welterweight title match, he won a clear victory over Cuba's Andres Aldama, who had beaten his first three opponents in two rounds or less. A few months later, Ray turned pro, beginning a career that would see him win an amazing four world championships.

The upper weight classes at Montreal were the private property of the Spinks brothers of St. Louis, Missouri. First Michael took the middleweight title by stopping Soviet Rufat Riskiev in the third round of their fight. Moments later, light heavyweight Leon entered the ring and disposed of Cuba's Sixto Soria in the third round too. The brothers both went on to great pro careers. Leon defeated Muhammad Ali for the world heavyweight championship less than two years after his Olympic triumph.

There was more, of course. Lightweight Howard Davis dedicated his Olympic performances to the memory of his mother, who died not long before the Games. His mom would have been proud; Howard won quickly and easily, earning a 5-0 decision over Romania's Simion Cutov, the European champion. Davis won the Val Barker Award as the Olympics' outstanding boxer. Add in the surprising flyweight title won by eighteen-year-old Leo Randolph over tough Cuban Ramon Duvalon and you know why the class of '76 will always be remembered as America's best.

Summer Games/Swimming

Spitz for the Gold

MARK SPITZ—1972—SEVEN GOLD MEDALS IN SWIMMING

As he stood on the starting block for the 200-meter butterfly at the 1972 Olympics in Munich, West Germany, American swimmer Mark Spitz thought about the challenge ahead of him. His goal: seven gold medals in one Olympics, a feat no one in Olympic history had accomplished. Could he be the first?

Things started well enough. Spitz led from start to finish in the 200-meter butterfly and set a world record. The same day, he anchored the U.S. 4 x 100-meter freestyle relay. Another gold, another world record. Two down and five to go.

It was more gold the following day. Mark set a third world record in the 200-meter freestyle. A few days later, Spitz won gold medals numbers 4 and 5 in the 100-meter butterfly and the 4 x 200-meter freestyle relay. Both were new world records.

Two to go. The toughest would be the 100-meter freestyle. Spitz owned the world record, but his teammate Jerry Heidenreich was at the top of his form. Rumors swept the Olympic Village that Spitz would skip the 100 meters. He didn't. Normally not a superfast starter, Mark was out of the blocks quickly and led at the turn. In the final 15 meters, Heidenreich began to close in. Spitz had just enough speed left to set his sixth world record and take first place.

One more to go. Mark swam the butterfly leg in the 4 x 100 medley relay. And, yes, the U.S. team set a world record. Spitz had accomplished his goal—seven golds!

Grace Under Pressure

SHANE GOULD—1972—WON ALL FIVE FREESTYLE SWIMMING EVENTS

At the 1972 Olympics in Munich, West Germany, while Mark Spitz was busy collecting men's swimming records, a fifteen-year-old from Australia was pulling off her own superfeat on the women's side. Shane Gould was the world-record holder in all five international freestyle swimming events. She hadn't lost a freestyle race in two years. She opened with a world record (2:23.07) in the 200-meter individual medley, catching strong East German Kornelia Ender in the final freestyle leg. In the 200-meter freestyle, she built up a huge lead, gave up about half of it, and then held off American Shirley Babashoff to set a world record at 2:03.56.

Next, Gould lined up for the 100-meter race against two supertough Americans. The U.S.'s Sandra Neilson got out quickly and led Shane through the first 50 meters. Gould couldn't close the gap. Then Babashoff rallied from seventh place, passing all the swimmers and leaving Shane in third with a bronze. Shane Gould's winning streak had ended; but her medal streak hadn't.

The following day, Gould was back in the water, determined to return to her gold-medal-winning ways. Did she ever! Her time of 4:19.44 in the 400-meter freestyle set a new world record by nearly two full seconds.

In Shane Gould's final event, the 800-meter freestyle, she took the silver medal, her fifth of the Games. Within eight days, the fifteen-year-old Gould swam twelve races, a total of 4,200 meters, and won five medals, three of them gold.

A year after her great Olympic moments, Shane Gould retired at age sixteen. The daily workout grind and the pressures of competitive swimming had sapped her strength. But while she was at the top of her game, nobody did it better.

Shooting Star

GERALD OUELLETTE—1956— PERFECT SCORE IN SMALL- BORE RIFLE

Success in small-bore rifle competition requires a steady hand, keen eyesight, and intense concentration. Most shooters don't even breathe when they shoot, since the slightest movement could ruin a shot. In the small-bore rifle event, shooters fire from 50 meters away from the target, and the bull's-eye is less than 1 inch in diameter.

That's what makes the perfect 60 out of 60 bull's-eyes by Canada's Gerald Ouellette at the 1956 Games in Melbourne, Australia, so remarkable. Ironically, the rifle used by Ouellette belonged to his teammate Gilmour Boa.

Ouellette was unhappy with his own weapon, so he asked Boa to share his rifle.

Boa went first, scored an impressive 598 points of a possible 600, then handed the rifle to Ouellette. With coaching from Boa, Ouellette got a perfect score.

But Ouellette's total, which won him a gold medal, did not go into the books as a world record. Unfortunately, Olympic officials had accidentally placed the targets 1 1/2 meters too close to the shooting line. But even if his record didn't count, Gerald Ouellette had his perfect Olympic moment.

Summer Games/Fencing

Staying Power

JANICE YORK ROMARY—1948-1968— FENCED IN MOST OLYMPICS

Carrying the American flag at the Olympics' opening ceremonies is a tremendous honor. In 1968 in Mexico City, Mexico, the honor went to Janice York Romary. Who?

Janice York Romary was never a superstar—her best finish was fourth place, and her sport, fencing, does not get a lot of attention.

"It was tough being a fencer," she remembers. "There were rarely any fencing results in the newspapers. My friends and family had to call me for the results." But Janice truly deserved the great honor of carrying the flag, because she accomplished something that no one else had ever done. From 1948 to 1968 she competed in six consecutive Olympiads. Now that is a feat!

Even after she retired, the Olympics beckoned one more time. At the 1984 Los Angeles Games, she was the fencing commissioner.

Summer Games/Gymnastics

The First Queen

LARISSA LATYNINA—1956-1964— WON THE MOST MEDALS: EIGHTEEN!

Russia's Larissa Latynina may not be a household name, but she provided gymnastics fans with dozens of great Olympic moments. She came on the scene in the 1956 Olympics in Melbourne, Australia, and by the time she completed the Rome Olympics in 1960 and the Tokyo Olympics in 1964, she had won an amazing eighteen medals! That's a record for any sport! Latynina set the standards which gymnasts still shoot for today.

Summer Games/Gymnastics

The Perfect 10s

NADIA COMANECI—1976—HIGHEST GYMNASTICS SCORE/FIRST PERFECT SCORE ON UNEVEN BARS

The tiny fourteen-year-old girl with the serious face flew across the uneven parallel bars. No one had ever seen anything like her. Her routine was daring and dangerous, and she was performing flawlessly. When Nadia Comaneci dismounted, the crowd went wild. But when her score was flashed on the board, they gasped in disbelief. A perfect 10! It had never been done before.

Where Olga Korbut, the most talked-about gymnast at the 1972 Games, was cute and perky, Romanian Nadia Comaneci was all business. She had been training for her Olympic moment since she was six years old. And when it finally arrived in Montreal, Canada, in 1976, she was ready.

The competition was stiff. Lyudmila Tourischeva, the 1972 all-around champion from the Soviet Union, was back to defend her crown. Tourischeva's teammates Nelli Kim and Olga Korbut were there as well. The Soviets had always dominated gymnastics, but now it was time for the Romanians to take over.

When all the scores were in, it wasn't even close. Nadia rang up an incredible seven perfect 10s on the uneven bars and the balance beam. She won the all-around gold medal.

She then went on to compete in the individual events. Nadia had two more 10s on the uneven bars, achieving the first perfect score of 20. She won the balance beam, over Korbut, with a near perfect score (19.95), and she also took the bronze in the floor exercises. The Comaneci legend was born.

The Powerhouse

MARY LOU RETTON—1984—FIRST AMERICAN TO WIN GYMNASTICS MEDAL

No American woman had ever won a medal in the Olympic gymnastics competition. In Los Angeles in 1984 there was a chance for gold—Mary Lou Retton. Mary Lou was behind Romanian Ecaterina Szabo by .05 points going into her last event— vaulting. Vaulting was Mary Lou's specialty.

Szabo's last event was the uneven bars. She did an excellent routine and received a nearly unbeatable score: 9.9. It looked as if Mary Lou would come in second. She needed a perfect 10 to win.

She zoomed down the runway, did a flashy Tsukahara vault, and stuck the landing. America waited for the score. It flashed up on the board—a perfect 10! Mary Lou had won!

Just for good measure, she did her second vault and got another 10!

As a result of the Soviet Union's boycott of the 1984 Games, the powerful Russian gymnastics team did not compete. Their absence opened up the field for the American girls. In the team competition, Retton led the U.S. to a second-place finish behind the talented Romanians. It was the American team's first medal since a bronze in 1948. By the time the Games were over, Mary Lou had also won a silver in the individual vault and bronzes in the floor exercise and uneven bars.

Americans took their champion into their hearts. In a sport where no American woman before her had ever won any kind of individual medal, Mary Lou had won four in two days.

The Streak Begins

U.S. BASKETBALL TEAMS UNBEATEN FOR THIRTY-SIX YEARS

When the United States met Canada for the first Olympic basketball gold medal game—in Berlin, Germany, in 1936—the court was outdoors and made of dirt. Rain turned the playing surface to mud. The final score was 19 to 8! The U.S. won.

It was nothing like basketball today. There was no shot clock; outside shooting wasn't anything like it is today; dunk shots were practically unheard of; and the game was stopped after every basket for a jump ball between the two centers. Add in the muddy court and the rain, and you can see why the two teams combined for only 27 points.

Nevertheless, the low-scoring rout was very important. It started the United States on one of the longest sports winning streaks ever. It lasted for thirty-six years! (See page 114 to see how the streak finally ended.)

What a Comeback!

TENNIS BACK ON OLYMPIC SCHEDULE—1988

How about this for a superfeat—a comeback after sixty-four years? That's what happened with the sport of tennis.

From the start of the modern Olympics, tennis was part of the program. World-famous stars, such as the U.S.'s Vincent Richards and Helen Wills and France's Henri Cochet and Suzanne Lenglen, performed on the court for their countries. But because there were so many other international championship tournaments, tennis was dropped from the Olympics after 1924.

Tennis officials were upset. Almost every other worldwide sport was part of the Olympics—why not tennis? It took sixty- four years to get tennis back on the schedule—the longest absence of any Olympic sport.

When it finally reappeared—in 1988 at Seoul, South Korea, it was tennis at its best. Not surprisingly, the game's world-class stars dominated. West Germany's Steffi Graf, arguably the best woman player in the world, and Czechoslovakia's Miloslav Mecir took the singles crowns. The U.S.'s top doubles teams, Ken Flach and Robert Seguso for the men and Pam Shriver and Zina Garrison for the women, also took home gold.

Tennis had returned to the Olympics with a bang!

Gable Clinches It

DAN GABLE—1972—WON WRESTLING GOLD

Every once in a while, a country will produce an athlete who totally dominates his sport. Dan Gable, the American wrestler, was like that. Between 1963 and 1973, Gable racked up a record of 299 wins, 6 losses, and 3 draws. Incredible.

But could he strike gold at the Olympics? You bet!

In 1972, at Munich, Germany, twenty-three-year-old Dan Gable from Waterloo, Iowa, won the gold medal in freestyle lightweight wrestling to cap his fabulous career. Gable was the first American to win this wrestling division since Shelby Wilson in 1960.

Gable was one of the most dedicated athletes in the sport— he trained seven hours a day, every day, for three years before the Munich Games. And in 1984, he served as coach of the U.S. freestyle wrestling team.

The Strongest Man

WEIGHT LIFTER VASSILY ALEXEYEV —1972-1976—LIFTED THE MOST

At the 1972 Games in Munich, West Germany, Russia's Vassily Alexeyev proved to the world that he was indeed the "strongest man at the Games" when he lifted more than four and a half times his own weight!

There was no competition for the thirty-year-old weight-lifting champion in the super heavyweight division that year. Alexeyev, who weighed in at 337 pounds, lifted 1,410 3/4 pounds! He had lifted 66.15 pounds more than the second-place finisher. And he was spotted later on having a breakfast of twenty-six fried eggs and a steak!

Alexeyev returned to the Olympics in 1976 (now weighing 345 pounds) and again was unchallenged, winning the gold medal easily. No person has ever dominated the sport of Olympic weight lifting the way Vassily Alexeyev did in 1972 and 1976.

Speed-Skating Queen

LYDIA SKOBLIKOVA—1964—FIRST TO WIN SIX WINTER GOLDS

Some years, all the great moments in a sport belong to one super athlete. That's the way it was in Innsbruck, Austria, in 1964, in women's speed skating. The Games belonged to Lydia Skoblikova of the Soviet Union. A double gold-medal winner at the 1960 Winter Games at Squaw Valley, California, the Russian schoolteacher came to Innsbruck looking for four more. No woman had ever won more than two golds in a single Winter Olympics.

With her biggest rival, teammate Inga Voronina, sidelined with a stomach ailment, Skoblikova began her quest with the 500- meter event. Skoblikova's time of 45.0 seconds set a new Olympic record.

With one gold in the bank, Lydia set out to defend her title in the 1,500-meter race. She knocked nearly three seconds off her old Olympic mark and made it two-for-two. Next came the 1,000 meters. Skoblikova won her third. She was the first woman ever to win three gold medals at one Winter Olympics and the first person (man or woman) to win five total Winter golds.

But she still wasn't done. Her greatest moment came in the 3,000 meters. An unknown North Korean named Pil-Hwa Han gave Lydia all she could handle. For most of the race, the tiny

Han kept up with Skoblikova's pace. However, Han fell into second place during the final two laps, leaving Skoblikova out in front. The final count for Lydia Skoblikova read four 1964 golds and six career golds—a feat no other athlete, male or female, had ever accomplished before.

Eric the Great

ERIC HEIDEN—1980—FIRST TO WIN FIVE SPEED-SKATING GOLDS IN A SINGLE OLYMPICS

On the grounds of the Lake Placid High School, where the 1980 Olympic speed skating was held, American Eric Heiden became an overnight superstar. The United States hadn't had a clean sweep of all the speed-skating titles since the 1932 Games. But then along came the dynamic Heiden, whizzing to an unprecedented five gold medals in speed skating. In fact, he won every gold speed-skating medal available that year!

Eric Heiden did compete in the 1976 Games in Innsbruck, Austria, but he didn't get much notice. He finished seventh in the 1,500 meters and nineteenth in the 500 meters. However, over the next few years Eric made tremendous improvements in speed and style, and he developed muscular 29-inch thighs.

Heiden was the favorite going into the 1980 Games. He won the 500 meters, the 1,000 meters, and the 5,000 meters easily. But in the middle of the 1,500-meter race, Eric nearly fell. Yet he managed to keep up his speed and win the event.

Heiden took the night off before his final race to attend the U.S.-Soviet ice hockey match. Two friends from his hometown of Madison, Wisconsin, were playing in the match. Eric was excited by the U.S. victory—more excited than by his own victories. He had trouble falling asleep and ended up oversleeping the next morning. He grabbed a few pieces of bread for breakfast, rushed to the track, and calmly broke the world record in the 10,000 meters by over 6 seconds!

Eric Heiden was the first Olympic competitor, in any sport, summer or winter, to win five individual-event gold medals at a single Olympics (three of Mark Spitz's seven gold medals had been in relay events). And to make Eric's Olympics an even happier occasion, his sister, Beth Heiden, won a bronze medal in the women's 3,000 meters.

Winter Games/Skiing

Nuke 'Em!

MATTI NYKANEN—1984-1988—FIRST PERSON TO WIN BOTH SKI-JUMP EVENTS

"Matti Nykanen is the best jumper of the last 100 years," said Finland's ski-jump coach Matti Pulli. "In fact, he's the best ever."

Few ski-jump experts disagree. Ever since he won his first international junior championship at age seventeen in 1981, Nykanen has clearly dominated his sport. No one—ever—has matched Nykanen's ability to take off from the bottom of the ramp and simply fly down the course.

Ski jumping isn't like long jumping. Distance alone doesn't get it done. Points are awarded for both distance and style. Although the skiers are frequently in the air for more than the length of a football field, if they get out of control in the air it doesn't matter how long the jump is. Poor style points will ruin their scores.

Nykanen's ability to fly far while under total control is what makes him a winner. At age twenty in the 1984 Games at Sarajevo, Yugoslavia, Matti took a gold medal on the 90-meter hill and a silver on the 70-meter. In Calgary, Canada, in '88, he was even better, sweeping both events and leading Finland to the first 90-meter team championship. How impressive was Matti's performance? Until he pulled off the ski-jump double at Calgary, Canada, no country, much less a single athlete, had ever won both events in the ski-jump competition in a single Olympics. Now that's super!

Love Match

IRINA RODNINA AND ALEKSANDR ZAITSEV—1976-1980—PAIRS FIGURE-SKATING GOLDS

In 1972, the Russian pairs-skating team of Irina Rodnina and Aleksey Ulanov won the Olympic gold medal. However, all was not as happy with this pair as it should have been after such a big victory.

Aleksey Ulanov was in love with Lyudmila Smirnova, who, with her partner Andrei Suraikin, was the Olympics pairs silver medalist. Ulanov found it difficult to compete against the woman he loved. The result was the breakup of Rodnina and Ulanov. Ulanov married Smirnova, and a nationwide search began to find a new partner for Irina Rodnina. The winner was Aleksandr Zaitsev of Leningrad.

In the World Championships in 1975, Rodnina-Zaitsev won the gold. This new pair had not only clicked on the ice as skaters, but also became husband and wife. They won the 1976 Olympic title and continued to win world championships, even after Irina gave birth to a baby.

But the 1980 Olympics in Lake Placid were going to be difficult; they had to compete against the strong American pair of Tai Babilonia and Randy Gardner. In the warm-up right before the competition, Randy fell four times because of a groin injury and the Americans were forced to pull out. Rodnina and Zaitsev skated flawlessly, and for the second straight time won the first-place votes of all nine judges. Irina Rodnina had matched the accomplishments of Sonja Henie by winning ten world championships and three Olympic golds.

Double Delight

EDDIE EAGAN—1920 & 1932—WINS A GOLD IN BOTH THE SUMMER AND WINTER OLYMPICS

It takes a lot of talent and work to make it to the Olympics in just one sport. But to master two different sports, one in winter and the other in summer, *and* win gold medals in both of them is more than unusual—it's extraordinary! Only one man has ever done it.

American Eddie Eagan began his trip to the Olympic record book by capturing a gold medal in the 1920 Games at Antwerp, Belgium. As a light-heavyweight boxer, he scored a final-round decision over Sweden's Sverre Sorsdal.

But that wasn't enough for the competitive Eagan. When the 1932 Winter Games were scheduled for Lake Placid, New York, Eagan became interested in the bobsled. He made the four-man U.S. team and took first place, winning the winter gold as well!

CHAPTER TWO
WEIRD
MOMENTS

The unexpected, the strange, even the comical . . .
some Olympic moments are just plain weird.

The First U.S. Games

It didn't take long after the start of the modern
Olympics for the Games to come to America. The
year was 1904 and the place was St. Louis, Missouri. The Olympics are supposed to be a great
international gathering, but the 1904 Olympics
did not work out that way.

Most of the countries of the world simply
didn't send any athletes. It was too difficult—and
expensive—to get to Missouri from Europe. Even
the founder of the Olympics, Baron Pierre de
Coubertin, didn't bother to show up.

Naturally, the results were a bit one sided.
The Americans dominated. In track and field
alone, the U.S. won seventy of the seventy-five
medals that were awarded.

The "Odd" Games

When the modern Olympics began in 1896, they ran like clockwork. Every four years, the world's best athletes gathered to celebrate the glory of sports. (At least, that was the goal.) And so the every-four-years games were held in 1896, 1900, 1904, 1906, 1908 . . .

Hey, wait a minute. Wasn't it supposed to be every four years? How did 1906 get in there?

Good question. The Olympics had started brightly enough in Athens in 1896, but then trouble surfaced. The 1900 Games in Paris were terribly disorganized and the equipment was horrible. (The track wasn't even level!) Most countries didn't send teams to the 1904 Games in St. Louis and, as a result, the Games were in trouble.

Enter the folks from Athens who had done such a great job at the opening Games of 1896. "Let us do it again in 1906," they said. And Olympics founder Baron de Coubertin agreed. The 1906 Athens Games turned out to be the perfect cure for what ailed the Olympics. There was more international competition; the medals were spread among many nations; and huge enthusiastic crowds packed the stadiums.

Marathon Madness

The grueling marathon, 26 miles and 385 yards of pain, is famous for weird moments. Take, for example, the story of Dorando Pietri's marathon at the 1908 Games in London, England.

Pietri, from a remote village in Italy, was practically unknown as the 1908 marathon began. Several English runners and American Johnny Hayes were the clear-cut favorites.

When the race began, the British runners took off quickly. Too quickly. Midway through the race, they had burned themselves out. Pietri kept dogging the leaders.

After 18 miles, South Africa's Charles Hefferon was in the lead, 3 minutes ahead of Pietri, who was still fairly fresh. At the 24-mile mark, Hefferon made a crucial mistake. Pietri was closing the gap steadily and Hefferon was exhausted. The South African drank a cupful of champagne to pick him up. Instead, the drink gave him stomach cramps and made him dizzy. With about a half-mile to go, Pietri zipped into the lead.

But Pietri began running too fast too soon. The louder the crowd along the London streets cheered for him, the faster he went. He would pay the price later.

Suddenly, the stadium loomed up ahead. Though he was just about out of gas, he plodded on. When he entered the arena, only the final 385 yards remained to be covered. Victory seemed to be his. But, without warning, he began to stagger. He headed the wrong way. He fell, got up, and fell again. The crowd watched in horror.

American Johnny Hayes was shortening the gap, but he seemed to have no chance if Pietri could stay on his feet. Pietri couldn't. Just as he was falling for the fifth time, Hayes came striding into the stadium. The previous day there had been bad blood between the Americans and British. The outcome of the 400-meter dash was argued for hours. So when British marathon director Jack Andrew saw Hayes about to win, he picked Pietri up and carried him across the line. He wanted to see anyone but an American win the race. The Italian flag was quickly raised on the victory pole. Thirty-two seconds later, a confused Hayes crossed the line.

American officials filed an immediate protest—and were upheld. Hayes was finally declared the winner, but people still talk about the amazing marathon of Dorando Pietri.

And Leave the Driving to Us

On a blistering-hot afternoon in St. Louis, Missouri, in 1904, the marathon leader, Fred Lorz of New York, arrived at the finish line looking fresh and rested. Too fresh in fact. Turns out the New Yorker had run the first 9 miles in the 26.2-mile race, then leaped into a car for the next 11. Fred then finished the race on foot, leaving the rest of the field in the dust.

When race officials figured out the truth, Lorz was instantly disqualified.

Ringing Defeat

It's not easy for athletes to accept defeat, especially Olympic defeat. But there are some athletes who deal with losing better than others.

In 1964 in Tokyo, for example, Spain's Valentin Loren was disqualified in the second round of his first featherweight contest. The referee ruled that Loren had ignored his warnings to stop holding his opponent and hitting him with an open glove. Both are violations of boxing rules. It was the end of the fight—but not the end for Loren. As soon as the decision was announced, the fighter "filed" his own protest, decking the referee with a flurry of hard rights and lefts. As a result, Loren was banned from amateur boxing for life.

And then on the same day, South Korean flyweight Dong-Kih Choh was disqualified in the second round of his bout. It seemed that Choh was holding his head too low which, according to Olympic boxing rules, is dangerous (to the boxer himself) and against the rules. Choh wasn't happy with this call either. He held his own private demonstration, a sit-in in the middle of the ring—holding up the boxing events for fifty-one minutes!

Losing Large

In the Olympics, there are losers and there are losers. But the all-time loser has to be Czecho-slovakia's Otomar Bures.

At the 1936 Berlin Games, Bures, a lieuten-ant in the Czech army, was entered in the eques-trian events. In equestrian events the riders start with a perfect score, then gain penalty points for a variety of reasons. The lowest score wins. Pen-alty points usually mount up into the hundreds. Usually.

Bures and his trusty steed, Mirko, really lit up the scoreboard. They managed to pile up more than 18,130 penalty points! In the 8-kilometer cross-country event, the judges set a time limit of 17 minutes and 46 seconds. Somehow, Otomar and Mirko took 2 hours, 46 minutes, and 36 sec-onds. They must have stopped for a really long lunch!

When Shorter Ran Longer

As wiry Frank Shorter waited at the starting line for the marathon at the 1972 Munich Games, he knew that it had been sixty-four years since an American had last won the Olympic marathon. He also knew that given his best shot, he could break the long losing streak.

Shorter decided to make his move early in

the race. He sprinted away from the pack and took a comfortable lead. But as he entered the stadium for the run to the finish line, Shorter heard boos and jeers. When he looked up, he saw another runner nearing the finish line! He couldn't figure out what was going on. It turned out that an imposter, Norbert Sudhous, had run onto the stadium track at the last moment. Sudhous was cruising along when the Olympic officials had him removed from the track and Shorter won.

The Fight That Wasn't

At the 1952 Olympics in Helsinki, Finland, Swedish boxer Ingemar Johansson was an immediate crowd favorite as he cruised into the heavyweight finals.

But his finals opponent, American Ed Sanders, was awesome: three Olympic fights, three punishing knockouts. What could Johansson do? He decided to play a defensive game. From the opening bell, Ingo backpedaled all the way, staying out of Sanders's range. Unfortunately, he forgot to throw even a single punch. Weird! Following the rules, the referee stopped the bout and disqualified the Swede for "not giving his best." As a result, he could not even receive the silver medal he earned by finishing second in the Olympic tournament.

Johansson returned home to Sweden in disgrace. But later he turned pro and became the heavyweight champion of the world. In fact, he had such a great pro career that in 1982 the Olympic committee presented him with his 1952 silver medal.

Floating Tires

When the West German four-man pursuit bike-racing team showed up for their gold medal match-up with the Soviets at Montreal, Canada, in 1976, they wore new tight one-piece silk racing suits. "Forget about it," said cycling officials. They instructed the quartet to change clothing; the special suits would give them an unfair advantage.

But losing that edge, the Germans had another trick up their sleeves. They filled their bicycle tires with lighter-than-air helium. Was that enough? You bet. The Germans finished the 4,000-meter race in 4:21.06, more than 6 seconds ahead of the Soviets.

The Long Wait

When British middleweight boxer Christopher Finnegan won a 3-2 decision over Russian Aleksei Kisselyov to win the boxing gold medal at Mexico City, Mexico, in 1968, he thought he had overcome every challenge. But there was one more challenge left, perhaps his toughest.

Olympic drug testing procedures required the British bricklayer to furnish a cup of urine for a postmatch checkup. But after his mighty ring effort, Finnegan couldn't deliver. No test, no gold, said Olympic officials. So Finnegan went to work on his final problem.

Four pints of beer didn't help. Neither did numerous cups of warm tap water. Cold water didn't do it either. Finnegan's coaches tried talking to him in the locker room. Forget it. He went to the TV studios and did a couple of interviews. Still he couldn't produce.

So he decided to go to dinner—accompanied by the Olympic boxing supervisors, of course. Finally at 1:40 in the morning, six hours after the action in the ring ended, Finnegan delivered, at last. The test was negative and the gold, finally, was his.

The Tropical Icemen

Think of the island of Jamaica: palm trees, beaches, warm water, bobsleds. *Bobsleds?*

Bobsleds and Jamaica just do not belong together. But there they were in Calgary, Canada, at the '88 Games. A smart promoter who realized that every country has a right to field an Olympic team put together a bobsled team, and they were the hit of the Games.

The foursome had to raise their own money to make the trip. So they sold colorful sweatshirts and even tapes of their theme song, which included the lyrics "We be trainin', gainin', strainin', and painin', but we ain't complainin'."

They were cool, all right, until it was time to hit the bobsled run. Their sled overturned and careened down toward the finish line after tossing its passengers headfirst into the wall of ice.

Fortunately, the Jamaicans escaped with only minor bumps and bruises and, as they walked down to the end of the course, they high-fived spectators all along the way.

Scales of Injustice

Pascual Perez couldn't believe that the Olympic officials at the 1944 Games in London, England, would not let him box because he was too fat. The flyweight boxer from Argentina knew he weighed less than the required 112 1/2 pounds. But the Olympic officials insisted that their records stated that he was overweight.

It seems that boxing officials had mistakenly weighed in one of Perez's Argentine teammates, a 119-pound bantamweight, in his place. When the mistake was discovered, Perez enjoyed the fastest 6 1/2-pound weight loss in world history.

Justice Delayed

Somebody obviously had cut math class and it nearly cost American ski jumper Anders Haugen an Olympic bronze medal. At the 1924 Games in Chamonix, France, the great Thorleif Haug of Norway took third place in ski jumping, with Haugen just missing a medal in fourth place.

Many years later, Haugen ran into silver medalist Narve Bonna. "You know you were gypped back in 1924," said Bonna. "My coaches told me that when they added up the scores, you finished third. The officials goofed." Together, the two old-timers let the International Olympic Committee (IOC) in on their discovery. Justice was finally done.

Fifty years after the competition ended in France, the IOC corrected the 1924 error. At a special ceremony in Oslo, the eighty-three-year-old Haugen received his bronze medal.

Almost Instant Replay

The year is 1948; the place London, England. The American track team has just breezed to victory in the 4 x 100-meter relay. But the gold goes to the British team!

Officials rule that the first U.S. runner handed the baton to teammate Lorenzo Wright outside the legal passing zone. "We did not," the American team protests. "Let's watch the video-tape!" Wait a minute. They couldn't have said that. This was 1948. Instant replay and video-tape hadn't been invented yet!

Enter famous filmmaker J. Arthur Rank. Rank's group was filming all of the Olympic events for a feature movie. The protest committee took one look at Rank's film and clearly saw that the Americans' baton-pass was entirely legal. Reluctantly, the English team passed their gold medals to the victorious U.S. quartet. You could call this the first use of instant replay—except it wasn't exactly instant. It took *three days* for the film to arrive!

Pressure Cooker

Skiing events are won and lost by fractions of a second, but it took French superstar Jean-Claude Killy seven hours to win his race. As the 1968 Winter Games unfolded at Grenoble, France, Killy was under the gun to produce an Alpine skiing triple: the downhill, the slalom, and the giant slalom.

The day started well enough. Killy took the downhill in 1:59.85. Victory in the giant slalom came even more easily. Now, only the slalom stood between Jean-Claude and skiing's biggest prize.

It wasn't easy. The course was shrouded in fog, making skiing especially challenging. But, in what must have been a special sign to the Frenchman, the sun came out for the brief time he was competing on the mountain. And then he got another lucky break. Norway's Hakon Mjon zipped down the hill faster than Killy, but the judges ruled that he had missed two gates. Mjon was disqualified.

Then came Austrian superstar Karl Schranz. Midway down the course, a misguided spectator suddenly appeared on the hill. Schranz stopped, brought the stranger to the judges, and asked for another chance. His request was granted. When Schranz reached the bottom of the hill, his time was better than Killy's. He won the gold. French fans mourned. But two hours later, it was ruled that Schranz *also* had missed a pair of gates on his first run, before the spectator ever got in his way. He too was disqualified.

But that wasn't the end of the story. Schranz protested, claiming he missed the gates because he saw the spectator up ahead. The appeals committee met for five hours before deciding, 3-2, that Killy was the winner.

Triple Tie

Ever wonder why so many race times are given in hundredths, and even thousandths, of a second? With modern electronic equipment, such timing is a snap. But what prompted Olympic officials to turn to high-tech timing took place during the 1968 Winter Games in Grenoble, France.

In the 500-meter speed-skating race, Russia's Lyudmila Titova was the winner in 46.1 seconds. But who finished second? Take your pick. The U.S.'s Dianne Holum, Mary Meyers, and Jennifer Fish were all timed at 46.3 seconds.

55

The officials had no other choice than to award each of them a silver medal. It must have been pretty crowded on the winner's stand!

WOULD YOU BELIEVE . . . ?

• Only five countries have been at all of the Summer Games since 1896: Australia, France, Greece, Great Britain, and Switzerland. And, of these, only Great Britain has been present at all the Winter Games as well.

• The largest crowd at any Olympic site was 150,000 at the 1952 ski jump in Oslo, Norway.

• The youngest-ever gold medalist was an unknown boy in Paris, France, in 1900. In the pairs rowing final, the coxswain for the Dutch crew was found to be too heavy (the coxswain steers the boat and needs to be very light). A small French boy was found at the last moment to cox the crew, and he helped them win the event. The boy's name was never written down, and he disappeared without a trace afterwards. But he was no more than ten years old and possibly as young as seven.

• The youngest female medalist was American Marjorie Gestring at age thirteen years, 268 days, in the 1936 women's springboard diving event.

• The heaviest Olympic competitor ever was freestyle super-heavyweight wrestling bronze medalist Chris Taylor from the U.S. He weighed 412 pounds!

• The tallest-ever player in Olympic basketball and the tallest-ever medalist in any sport was American Tommy Burleson, who won in 1972 and measured 7 feet, 4 inches!

• There was no time limit in wrestling bouts until 1924. In 1912, the Greco-Roman middle-weight bout between Russian Martin Klein and Finland's Alfred Asikainen lasted for 11 hours, 40 minutes! Klein won.

• The first Olympic marriage took place right after the 1920 Games in Antwerp, Belgium, when American diver Alice Lord and high-jump champion Dick Landon tied the knot.

• The first gold medals won by a husband and wife were won by Ludovika and Walter Jakobsson of Finland for pairs figure skating at Antwerp in 1920.

• The first brothers to win track and field medals at the same Olympics were Platt and Ben Adams of the U.S., who came in first and second in the 1912 standing high jump.

• The first time women were allowed to compete in the Olympics was in 1900 in Paris, but their participation was limited to tennis and golf. The first female gold medalist was Britain's Charlotte Copper, who won the tennis singles title.

• The highlight of the 1904 Olympics was an event called the "plunge for distance," in which the swimmers competed to see how far they could dive in and swim underwater.

● One of the most popular Olympic events from 1900 to 1920 was the tug-of-war. The most famous Games tug-off occurred at the 1908 London Olympics, when the London police (representing England) finally got the best of the Stockholm police (representing Sweden). There is no report on how long it took the English to pull the Swedes over the line.

Summer Games – 1932 – Los Angeles, U.S.A./*Babe Didrikson prepares to throw the javelin for a new world record.*

Winter Games – 1968 – Grenoble, France/*Frenchman Jean-Claude Killy races down the slalom course to win all the alpine skiing events.*

Summer Games – 1972 – Munich, West Germany/
Cuban Teofilo Stevenson (in the blue trunks), the first boxer to win three heavyweight gold medals in a row, throws a powerful right hook.

Summer Games – 1976 – Montreal, Canada/*All-around gold medalist Nadia Comaneci scores a perfect 10 on the balance beam.*

© Focus On Sports

Summer Games – 1936 – Berlin, Germany/*The 1936 Olympics saw Jesse Owens run away with four gold medals!*

Summer Games – 1972 – Munich, West Germany/ *Russian Vassily Alexeyev — "the strongest man in the world" — lifts 1,410 3/4 pounds!*

Winter Games – 1980 – Lake Placid, U.S.A./*America's Eric Heiden powers around the rink to win five speedskating golds.*

Summer Games – 1972 – Munich, West Germany/
Perfect balance — Olga Korbut captures the hearts of gymnastics fans around the world.

Summer Games – 1988 – Seoul, South Korea/*One-handed pitcher Jim Abbott winds up for the winning pitch.*

Summer Games – 1988 – Seoul, South Korea/*Greg Louganis is the first diver to take home gold in both the springboard and platform events two Olympics (1984 & 1998) in a row. Here he executes a perfect springboard dive.*

Summer Games – 1976 – Montreal, Canada/*American Edwin Moses leaps to a record-breaking finish in the "killer" 400-meter hurdles.*

Winter Games – 1976 – Innsbruck, Austria/_The graceful Dorothy Hamill skates flawlessly for the gold._

CHAPTER THREE
AGAINST ALL ODDS

The Olympics are full of personal drama—stories of people who had to summon incredible courage and overcome misfortune to reach their moments of Olympic glory.

The Jumper

RAY EWRY—1900-1908—TRACK AND FIELD

The Olympic Games are always filled with stories of incredible achievement over impossible odds. Take Ray Ewry, an American track star from nearly a hundred years ago.

The fact that Ray Ewry could even walk was a miracle. Ray had had polio as a child. He was paralyzed and could get around only in a wheelchair. Doctors said that the chair might be his home for life, but Ray didn't buy it. He was determined not to allow his body to waste away. He forced himself to exercise his paralyzed legs, and he learned to walk. Ray then began a strict routine of jumping exercises to strengthen his legs. He became an amazing jumper and jumped right into Olympic history.

On July 16, 1900, Ray Ewry competed at the Olympics in Paris, France. He was entered in three now discontinued events—the standing high jump, standing long jump, and standing hop, step, and jump. The twenty-six-year-old Ewry won all three gold medals, setting a world record in the standing high jump (5 feet, 5 inches) in the process.

But he wasn't through. In St. Louis, Missouri, in 1904, he repeated his amazing triple, setting a new world mark in the standing long jump (11 feet, 4 7/8 inches). And though the standing triple jump was dropped after the 1904 Games, Ray won gold medals in his other two events at both the off-year Olympics in Athens, Greece, in 1906 and again in London, England, in 1908.

Ray Ewry's never-give-up attitude won him ten Olympic gold medals and a place in history as a symbol of the true Olympic spirit!

Local Call

DUNCAN MCNAUGHTON—1932— TRACK AND FIELD

Canadian high jumper Duncan McNaughton had a tough way to go to get to the Olympics. But he proved that sometimes Olympic spirit and nerve are just as important as talent. McNaughton's objective was to be included in Canada's 1932 Olympic team. He was good—but apparently not good enough for Canadian officials to award him a spot on the roster. So he appealed to the organizers on a money basis, saying he was a bargain!

"I attend the University of Southern California in Los Angeles," McNaughton told them, "and that's where the Olympics are being held. It won't cost you a nickel to get me there."

At the last moment, Canadian officials finally caved in and let McNaughton on the team. It was their best decision ever. McNaughton's leap of 6 feet, 5 1/2 inches won him (and his team) a gold medal!

The Flying Housewife

FANNY BLANKERS-KOEN—1948— TRACK AND FIELD

Fanny Blankers-Koen of the Netherlands is often called the greatest female track and field star of all time. And it's not *just* because she won four gold medals in one Olympics. How (and when) she did it is even more amazing.

Fanny entered her first Olympics in 1936 in Berlin, Germany. She was eighteen years old. She managed only a tie for sixth place in the high jump, but she knew she'd have another chance in 1940. But World War II cancelled the 1940 and 1944 Olympic Games, so Fanny's next chance didn't come until 1948. By that time, she was over thirty years old, married to her coach, and the mother of two children. Now, thirty may be young in most careers, but for a track star, thirty is old. The odds—and the years—were certainly against Fanny Blankers-Koen, but the crowd was on her side. Everyone was rooting for the "Marvelous Mama," as she was called. Though she excelled at many different events, as a woman Fanny was limited to only three events plus a relay, according to Olympic rules at the time. (Officials wanted to protect the "weaker" sex.)

Fanny was perfect. She won the 100 meters (11.9 seconds), won the first-ever 200 meters (24.4 seconds), and set a new Olympic record (11.2 seconds) in taking the 80-meter hurdles. Then she anchored Holland's 4 x 100-meter relay team to victory in 47.5 seconds. Were it not for the limiting rule, there's no telling how many medals she would have won, because Fanny just happened to be the world-record holder in two events she couldn't fit into her schedule: the high jump and long jump. Pretty good for an "old lady"!

Wonderful Wilma

WILMA RUDOLPH—1960—TRACK AND FIELD

Wilma Rudolph weighed only 4 1/2 pounds at birth. She was crippled by illness at age four. She spent the next three years in bed! She was seven by the time she learned how to walk properly. Yet Wilma Rudolph is one of the greatest track stars in Olympic history.

The twentieth of twenty-two children of a poor Tennessee family ("I learned to run fast so

I could get to the table first," she once joked), she found that she could run with ease. She won her first American amateur championship at age fifteen. The following year, she was off to Melbourne, Australia, as part of the 1956 Olympic team. She won a bronze medal in the 4 x 100-meter relay. But that didn't satisfy Wilma. She made up her mind that 1960 would be her year.

It was. She was the darling of the Games in Rome, Italy, with her graceful, floating running style. She was so relaxed that she took a nap in the locker room before the 100-meter semifinals. But she certainly wasn't napping on the track. She won her semifinals by 3 yards in 11.3 seconds, then came back in a wind-aided 11 seconds flat to win the finals—and the gold—again by an impressive 3 yards.

The 200 meters produced more of the same. Wilma set an Olympic record by running 23.2 seconds in her opening heat. Then she beat Germany's Jutta Heine by 4 yards in the finals in 24 seconds flat.

She still wasn't finished. No American woman had ever won three gold medals in one Olympics. But that's what Wilma was going for. If the American team could win the 4 x 100-meter relay, she'd have her third gold. The team was strong. They had a good chance—then, disaster! A sloppy final baton pass left Wilma tied with her German rival Heine as they started the final leg. It was up to Wilma. She put on one last push, pulled away and beat the odds again. Wilma Rudolph brought home the gold.

Switch-Hitter

KAROLY TAKACS—1948—
PISTOL SHOOTING

Call it the greatest comeback ever. Call it the most courageous performance of all time. Call it heroic. Call it amazing!

A member of the outstanding Hungarian pistol team, Karoly Takacs was serving in the Hungarian army in 1938 when a hand grenade exploded in his right hand—his shooting hand. After such a near-fatal accident, most athletes would have walked away from a sport which required incredible steadiness and accuracy. Not Takacs.

When the Games resumed in London, England, in 1948 after World War II, there was Karoly Takacs, as a member of the Hungarian pistol team. Through sheer courage and hard work, Takacs was back—shooting left-handed.

Shoot? Did he ever! Karoly set an all-time world record of 580 points to win the gold. And he was back in Helsinki, Finland, in 1952. He edged out teammate Szilard Kun, 579-578, to win the medal again. To this day, Takacs's amazing comeback remains one of the most incredible stories in Olympic history.

The Horsewoman

LIS HARTEL—1952—EQUESTRIAN

In 1944, twenty-three-year-old Lis Hartel was one of Denmark's leading women equestrians. On a horse, her strength and coordination were remarkable. Then one morning, she arose with a stiff neck. Within days, doctors told Lis Hartel the terrible news: she had polio. She was paralyzed and would probably never walk again.

For years, Lis struggled to strengthen her muscles. She learned to walk with crutches. Her dreams of glory as an equestrian seemed to be gone forever. But no one had counted on Lis's great will. She insisted on riding a horse once again. It was difficult. When she started, she had to rest for weeks after every session on horseback. Amazingly, three years after being struck down by polio, she was able to compete in the Scandinavian riding championships.

In 1952 (the first year women were allowed to compete in Olympic dressage events), she was on Denmark's team. In dressage, riders are required to guide their horses through precise movements. Hartel still had to be helped on and off her horse, but on horseback she was in control. She won the silver medal. In eight years Lis Hartel had beaten her fiercest opponent—polio.

Snap! Crackle! Papp!

LASZLO PAPP—1948-1956—BOXING

Olympic boxing has always been a young man's game. But Hungary's Laszlo Papp showed that for some boxers the years can be good.

Papp debuted at the 1948 Games in London, England, winning a decision over hometown favorite John Wright to take the middleweight gold medal. He was back in 1952, in Helsinki, Finland, dropping South Africa's Theunis van Schalkwyk with a right hook in the final round, which broke open a close fight. Papp won the first Olympic light middleweight title and his second gold.

Amazing! But what is even more amazing is that Papp showed up in 1956 at Melbourne, Australia, ready to go for the gold again at the age of thirty.

No one thought he had a chance. But Laszlo Papp believed in himself. He won a decision from American Jose Torres, who later became the world professional light-heavyweight champion.

Laszlo Papp won three gold medals and a special place in the Olympic story.

Smokin' Joe

JOE FRAZIER—1964—BOXING

Joe Frazier's legendary battles with Muhammad Ali for the professional world heavyweight boxing title are still being talked about. But long before Smokin' Joe ruled the professional heavyweight division, there was the Olympics. And to win a precious gold medal, Joe needed a break, a little bit of luck, and a huge dose of courage.

In the U.S. Olympic trials in 1964, Frazier lost to Buster Mathis. That meant Mathis would go to the Olympics and Joe would have to wait four more years to get another chance. Mathis and Frazier fought in a pre-Olympics exhibition match. Mathis landed a right to Frazier's midsection and pulled back in pain. Mathis had broken his finger, and Frazier got his spot on the Olympic team. Joe was on his way to Tokyo.

Joe knew he'd been lucky and was determined to win. He floored his first two Olympic opponents with a powerful left hook. The early knockouts put Frazier into the medal race. In the semifinals, he faced the Soviet star, Vadim Yemelyamov, his toughest foe yet. Joe was up to the test. Twice he floored the Russian. Then, sensing a knockout, he moved in. A Frazier left hook wobbled Yemelyamov, but sent intense pain up Smokin' Joe's left arm. Just in time, the Russian threw in the towel. Post-fight X-rays showed that Frazier had broken his left hand with that crucial punch.

Would Joe drop out of the finals and settle for the silver medal? No way. Fighting mostly with his right hand, Joe won a narrow decision over Germany's Hans Huber. In one of the bravest shows in the history of Olympic boxing, Joe Frazier had earned his gold medal—the hard way.

Bouncing Back

GREG LOUGANIS—1988—DIVING

Greg Louganis of the United States was one of the greatest divers in the history of the sport. During the 1984 Games in Los Angeles, California, Greg had won both the springboard and platform diving titles in the same Olympics. And he arrived in Seoul, South Korea, for the 1988 Olympics, determined to be the first person to win both diving competitions in consecutive Olympics. He had no idea what was ahead of him.

It was the preliminary round of the springboard event. Greg Louganis stood at the end of the 3-meter diving board, about 10 feet above the water. Louganis took off on a reverse two and a half (a reverse dive with two and a half somersaults in the air). But something went wrong—Greg took off too close to the board and, on his way down, he hit his head on the edge. The crowd gasped as he fell awkwardly into the pool, his blood staining the water red.

Louganis left the pool deck in shock. "I didn't realize I was that close," he said. Talk about courage! After receiving four temporary stitches, Greg got right back on the board. He had to, or he would have lost his chance at the medal. Incredibly, his next dive was the best of the day— by anyone!

The next day the medal competition began, and all twelve finalists started from zero. Louganis knew his toughest competition would come from Tan Liangde of China. Right from the start, Louganis began to build a lead. It grew to 20 points when Tan was sloppy on the same reverse two and a half Louganis had "blown" the previous day. When it was over, Greg had beaten Tan by 26 points and bronze medalist Li Deliang, also of China, by 65.

When he wrapped up the platform title a few days later, Greg Louganis had done what no one had done before, winning Olympic diving's double double. And his display of courage was truly a great Olympic moment.

The One-Handed Pitcher

JIM ABBOTT—1988—BASEBALL

As Jim Abbott stood on the mound in Seoul, South Korea, and leaned in for the catcher's sign, he had to smile. Jim was born with a stump where his right hand should be. Yet here he was, pitching for the U.S. in the 1988 Olympic baseball championship game against Japan.

A star athlete at Flint (Michigan) High

School and the University of Michigan, the 6-foot, 3-inch left-hander became one of the U.S.'s most talented pitchers by the time he wrapped up his college career. The amateur baseball world hadn't seen anything like Abbott.

Already the first draft choice of the California Angels, Jim was fast—and smart. Even though he had to pitch with his glove under his right arm, pausing only briefly to put it on his left hand after the pitch, he was as effective as any pitcher in the Olympic tournament. Before the Games, he led the U.S. team on a summer tour, finishing 8-1 with a nifty 2.55 ERA. Then, in the biggest game of his life, in South Korea, Jim went all the way, allowing only seven hits, as the U.S. defeated Japan, 5-3, for the gold medal.

Abbott's next stop was Anaheim, California, where the California Angels had a uniform waiting for him. But on that day in Seoul, he was already in heaven.

Ruud Treatment

BIRGER RUUD—1932-1948— SKI JUMPING

Some say he was the best ski jumper ever. But even if others have passed him, Norway's Birger Ruud will always have a special place in sports— and world—history. At the first U.S. Winter Olympics, at Lake Placid, New York, in 1932— 20-year-old Ruud led a one-two-three Norwegian sweep in the 90-meter ski jump. Four years later, at the German twin cities of Garmisch-Partenkirchen, Ruud was the star again as Norway took three of the first four places. Only Sweden's Sven Eriksson slipped in at second place to prevent another Norwegian sweep.

When World War II began, Ruud and his ski-jumping brothers Sigmund and Asbjorn, were asked to cooperate with the Nazis. The Ruuds refused. They were sent to a concentration camp where they were held prisoner for several years.

After the war, Ruud was ready to pass on his knowledge to the next generation of ski jumpers. He became the coach of the Norwegian ski-jumping team at the 1948 Winter Olympics in St. Moritz.

The night before the 90-meter jump, the weather turned bad. Coach Ruud had tremendous confidence in his top two jumpers, but he was concerned that his third was not experienced enough.

So the next morning, Ruud called for a substitute: himself! Even though he was thirty-six years old and hadn't competed seriously for years, Ruud won the silver medal for his country. His teammates took first and third. It was another Norwegian sweep and an amazing triumph over incredible odds for Birger Ruud.

Great Scott!

SCOTT HAMILTON—1984—FIGURE SKATING

As the 1984 Winter Olympics opened in Sarajevo, Yugoslavia, almost every figure-skating expert agreed American Scott Hamilton would win the gold!

But fifteen years earlier, no one expected that Scott would be battling for any kind of world's championship. He was battling for his life! When he was about ten years old, he was in and out of hospitals with a mysterious illness. When other boys were growing out of their clothes, Scott had actually stopped growing. He was small and weak. Some doctors thought he would die. But experts at Children's Hospital in Boston finally determined that Scott had a problem with his digestive system, and they saved his life.

When he recovered, he was small for his age. But he discovered that he had natural skating ability. When his parents saw that he was serious about the sport, they got him the best teachers. Scott set his goal—the Olympics!

In the 1980 Olympics at Lake Placid, he took fifth place. That wasn't enough for Scott. His great Olympic moment came four years later—at Sarajevo.

At Sarajevo, he took first place in the opening-round compulsory figures and never gave up the lead. Canada's Brian Orser, another gifted skater, pressed him all the way. But in the end, Hamilton's athletic ability—his triple toe-loops, triple lutzes, and triple salchows—won him the gold.

Scott is only 5 feet, 3 1/2 inches tall, but he has proven with his bravery and determination that he is an Olympic giant.

CHAPTER FOUR
OLYMPIC PIONEERS

They were the first . . . the first to try something new . . . the first to push beyond what was expected. These pioneers have influenced all the Olympians who followed.

The Babe

BABE DIDRIKSON—1932—TRACK AND FIELD

Women have been competing in the Olympics since 1900, but it took one super athlete to really put women's sports on the map. It took "Babe."

The legend of Mildred "Babe" Didrikson began during the 1932 U.S. Olympic trials. At age twenty-one, she had already made a big name for herself as an All-American basketball player.

During the trials, Babe entered eight of the ten track and field events. She won six of them, scoring 30 points, 8 more than the *entire* University of Illinois team, which finished second!

What would she do at Los Angeles? Olympic rules for women in those days prevented her from entering more than three events. She started with the javelin. Though she reported that it slipped as she threw it, she fired it 143 feet, 4 inches. It was a new Olympic record.

Next came the 80-meter hurdles. Her time of 11.7 seconds set a world mark. Another gold for the Babe. Finally came the high jump. Babe had tied Jean Shiley at the Olympic trials and, at Los Angeles, they tied again at 5-5 1/4. Officials decided, however, that Babe had dived over the bar, her head crossing first. This was against the rules at that time. She had to settle for a silver. (Later rules permitted Didrikson's new jumping style.)

When the Olympics were over, Babe tried her hand—successfully—at other sports. Inspired by her husband, George Zaharias, she made golf her passion. At one point, she won fourteen straight tournaments, an unheard-of winning streak. A five-time U.S. Woman Athlete of the Year, she was voted the greatest athlete of the first half of the century. Babe Didrikson was an inspiration to every female athlete who came after her.

Queen of the Ice

SONJA HENIE—1924-1936— FIGURE SKATING

The figure-skating competition is always one of the great highlights of the Winter Olympic Games. But the creativity and excitement of a young woman named Sonja Henie made women's figure skating what it is today.

Sonja Henie was only eleven years old when she won her first Norwegian figure-skating championship and competed in her first Olympic Games. The daughter of one of Oslo's richest men, young Sonja captured the hearts of the fans at the first Winter Olympics in Chamonix, France, in 1924, even though she didn't come close to winning.

Four years later, at St. Moritz, Switzerland, Sonja won her first Olympic gold medal. She was fourteen, the youngest medal winner at the 1928 Games. The crowd and the judges had never seen a skater like her. She revolutionized women's skating by blending ballet movements into the usual routine of skating moves. She also added the first jumps to women's figure skating. When the news of this incredible Norwegian teenager spread, everyone in the world wanted to see her in action. Sonja immediately launched a U.S. and Canadian tour. She drew big crowds everywhere she went and brought more and more attention to figure skating.

But one Olympic gold and worldwide celebrity weren't enough. Sonja Henie came back to win again at Lake Placid in 1932. Then, at the 1936 Winter Games in Garmisch-Partenkirchen, Germany, she won an unmatched third victory. Overall she won 1,473 championships during her spectacular amateur career, and she changed the look of women's skating forever.

Right on the Button

DICK BUTTON—1948-1952—
FIGURE SKATING

These days, Americans rely on Dick Button for the inside scoop on figure skating. Whenever the skaters take the ice, the knowledgeable Button is on the sidelines, ready to explain every detail of every performance to the TV audience. But did you know that Dick Button was a figure-skating pioneer himself?

In 1948, as a Harvard University freshman, Button brought home his first gold. In the St. Moritz Games, Button executed an unheard-of double axel (two full rotations in the air with a difficult forward takeoff).

"I almost didn't try it," Button remembers. "I had a lead going into the final round and I didn't want to blow it. In the end, I convinced myself that just because it was the Olympics, I shouldn't chicken out. Besides, once I took the steps leading up to the double axel, I simply had to do it. It worked out beautifully."

Four years later, at the 1952 Games at Oslo, Norway, Button became the first skater to perform a triple loop. That move required him to complete three revolutions and a smooth landing on one foot, another all-time first.

The brand-new triple loop gave Button his second gold—and a permanent place in the history of figure skating.

Mr. and Mrs. Pairs

THE PROTOPOPOVS—1968— PAIRS SKATING

Pairs skating. Nobody really gave this Olympic sport much thought—that is, until the dynamic Soviet pair of Lyudmila and Oleg Protopopov came on the scene.

Before the Protopopovs, pairs skating was practically an "extra" event on the Olympic schedule. The moves were predictable and boring. The Protopopovs raised it to the same high level of interest as the men's and women's individual competition. They invented many new moves, including the terrifying "death spiral," in which the woman is spun around horizontally just a few inches above the ice, balancing on just the back inside edge of her skate blade.

The Protopopovs finished ninth in the 1960 Olympics at Squaw Valley, California. They were clearly disappointed and they returned to Russia more determined than ever to dominate their event. In 1964, they were ready. With a style never seen before, they took home the gold. And they won the gold again in 1968.

But points and medals don't begin to tell the story. As Oleg put it, "You cannot measure art by points. We skate from the heart. To us, it is the spiritual beauty that matters." To the many millions who watched them, that was easy to see.

The Flop That Wasn't

DICK FOSBURY—1968—TRACK AND FIELD

For decades, high jumpers cleared the bar by leaping off one foot, turning their bodies, and passing over the bar parallel to and facing the ground. There were various rolls and straddles, but the form was basically the same. And then came Dick Fosbury.

The young man from Oregon did a little studying, a little figuring, and invented a better way. Fosbury would race up to the bar, take off on his left foot, pivot his right leg back, and leap up, bending his back backward. His head crossed the bar first, followed by the rest of his body, with his legs kicking up and out of danger at the top of the leap.

The "Fosbury Flop" met with criticism. Track coaches and officials thought it was dumb, maybe even illegal. But it was legal and won him a spot on the 1968 U.S. Olympic Team.

At Mexico City, Mexico, rival coaches screamed about the new Fosbury Flop. But the crowds loved it. Fosbury missed once at 7 feet, 4 1/4 inches, then cleared that height, too. The Olympic record—and the gold medal—were his. By 1980, thirteen of the sixteen Olympic finalist were using the "crazy" Fosbury technique, and by the 1990s the Flop had produced a jump over 8 feet!

When Joan Flew

JOAN BENOIT—1984—TRACK AND FIELD

Tens of thousands of excited fans lined the streets in Los Angeles, California, in 1984. History was about to be made—the running of the first women's Olympic marathon. Olympic track and field officials had always stated that distance running was too much of a strain on a woman. Women didn't get to run 1,500 meters (a little less than 1 mile) in the Olympics until 1972. And they weren't given a 3,000-meter race until 1984. But for the first women's Olympic marathon—26 miles, 385 yards, all of the best runners in the world were on hand: American Julie Brown (the course record holder), Norway's world champion Grete Waitz, Ingrid Kristiansen of Norway (just back from having a baby), and U.S. world-record holder Joan Benoit.

The race itself was over quickly. After just a few miles, Benoit broke away from the pack. The other leaders decided to let her go. They figured she'd go too fast and slow down later, giving them an opportunity to pass her. That was a serious mistake. The veteran from Maine pulled away and just kept on going. She crossed the finish line 2:24:52 after she started, a minute and 66 seconds before any of the other stars. It was one of the most popular American victories of the Games and made Joan Benoit an Olympic pioneer.

CHAPTER FIVE
UNFORGETTABLE PERSONALITIES

Every Olympics has them—athletes whose personalities and style make as big an impression on the Games as their medals and records do.

Feats of Clay

CASSIUS CLAY—1960—BOXING

Many experts say that the most fascinating sports figure of modern times is ex-heavyweight boxing champion Muhammad Ali.

Ali, like so many other great athletes, first came to fame in the Olympics. He was a light-heavyweight boxer then. And his name was Cassius Marcellus Clay. The fast-talking, fast-punching Clay was the hit of the entire Olympic village at the 1960 Games in Rome, Italy. But his friendly spirit wouldn't do him a bit of good if he couldn't deliver in the ring. The road to the gold wasn't going to be easy.

The well-muscled youngster seemed up to the challenge. First he stopped Belgium's Yan Becaus in the second round of their bout. Then he quickly disposed of 1956 Olympic middleweight champion Gennady Schatkov of the Soviet Union and

Tony Madigan of Australia. In the final, Clay danced around Poland's Zbigniew Pietrzykowski for two rounds before jumping all over him in the third and final round. It wasn't even close.

Four years after taking the Olympic gold, Clay won the world heavyweight title in a shocking upset over champion Sonny Liston. And, after he changed his name to Muhammad Ali, he went on to more than fifteen years at the top of the heavyweight division. Although now retired and slowed down by Parkinson's disease, Muhammad Ali remains one of the world's most popular athletes.

The Russian Superstar

OLGA KORBUT—1972—GYMNASTICS

As the world watched, a tiny gymnast began her routine on the uneven parallel bars. But her foot touched the mat on her mount—a serious mistake. Her concentration was broken. She fell off the bars. Her routine was a disaster, and her chance at the all-around gold medal lost. Heartbroken, she went to the bench and cried. The whole world cried with her.

Who was this unknown pixie who had captured the hearts of millions? She was Olga Korbut, seventeen years old, 4 feet, 11 inches tall and weighing 85 pounds. She had two pigtails and an adorable smile. The world took one look at her and fell in love.

The next day, Olga was back, this time in the individual competition. This spirited girl refused to let the defeats of the day before bother her. She finished second to East Germany's Karin Janzon on the uneven bars. Then, to everyone's delight, she won two gold medals—on the balance beam and in the floor exercises.

Olga finished only seventh in the all-around, but that didn't matter. She singlehandedly started a worldwide gymnastics craze with her enormous appeal.

The Battle of Britain

STEVE OVETT AND SEBASTIAN COE—1980—TRACK AND FIELD

Simply put, Steve Ovett and Sebastian Coe didn't like each other. The two British distance runners didn't talk to one another and, for two years, they didn't compete against one another. They shared the world record for 1,500 meters; Ovett had recently taken the record for the mile away from Coe.

When the U.S. led a boycott of the 1980 Olympics in Moscow, interest in the track and field events dropped to near zero. The only saving grace: a hugely anticipated duel between two English distance runners, Ovett and Coe. Though their government had asked its athletes to stay at home, Ovett and Coe joined a handful of British athletes who decided to take part.

The scouting report indicated that Coe, the speed man, would win the 800 meters. Ovett, the strength man, was the choice in the 1,500 meters. So much for the experts. Ovett won the 800 in 1:45.4, barely holding off his archrival by half a second.

That set the stage for the 1,500 meters. Another surprise. Coe edged East Germany's Jurgen Straub and Ovett for the gold. Only six-tenths of a second separated the three.

Then, in the true spirit of the Olympics, Coe and Ovett embraced—and went to dinner together!

Flo Jo

FLORENCE GRIFFITH-JOYNER— 1988—TRACK AND FIELD

From the first time she set foot on the Olympic track in Seoul, South Korea, in 1988, everyone knew she was special. There were the long, polished fingernails. There were the colorful, one-legged tights and the racy, hooded bodysuits. And there was the smile, always the smile, as she raced toward the finish line.

But could she run? You bet she could.

Florence Griffith-Joyner, the wife of Olympian Al Joyner and the sister-in-law of world champion heptathlete Jackie Joyner-Kersee, always looked as if she were having fun on the track. Holder of the world record for 100 meters

(10.49 seconds), she prepared carefully for the 1988 Games in Seoul, knowing that Evelyn Ashford of the U.S. and Heike Drechsler of East Germany were potential threats.

In the end, there was no trouble at all. In her first heat in the 100 meters, Flo Jo broke Ashford's Olympic record by running 10.88. But Ashford wasn't through. She tied the new mark in her semifinals race. Flo Jo's response? She broke the record again, speeding through her 100 meters in 10.62. In the finals, it was Griffith-Joyner all the way in 10.54. That record didn't count, however, as the wind at her back was more than track rules allow.

Flo Jo continued breaking records. In the 200 meters, she set a new mark at 21.34. Finally, she helped the U.S. 4 x 100 relay team to a gold medal. For Florence Griffith-Joyner, who came to Seoul expecting to win, the results were better than she could have ever imagined.

The Doctor Is In

BENJAMIN SPOCK—1924— BOAT RACING

Many people who later went on to great success in other areas had their first taste of glory at the Olympics. At the Paris Games in 1924, a lanky 6-foot, 4-inch Yale University junior named Ben Spock was one of nine Americans in the eight-oared shell with coxswain. Spock and his teammates performed perfectly, leading the runner-up Canadian shell by nearly 16 seconds to win the gold medal.

Does the name Ben Spock ring a bell? What about Dr. Benjamin Spock, M.D.? His successful *Common Sense Book of Baby and Child Care* was—and is—the source of child-rearing information for millions of parents all over the world and has helped to raise thousands of children— maybe even you!

Young Blood and Guts

GEORGE S. PATTON—1912—TRACK AND FIELD

Most Americans never heard of George S. Patton, Jr., until the key battles of World War II. But sports fans knew all about him back in 1912, when he competed in the modern pentathlon in the Olympics in Stockholm, Sweden.

The future heroic general, who eventually became known as "Old Blood and Guts," met the world's best in five grueling events: shooting, swimming (a 300-meter race), fencing, cross-country riding, and cross-country running. Patton wound up in the top seven in four of the five events. Oddly enough, it was a disappointing twenty-first-place finish in shooting that cost Patton a medal. But Patton, then a lieutenant, showed the Army that they had one tough athlete on their roster by finishing fifth all-around.

The Royals

Members of various European royal families have always been involved in the Olympics. Most of them have been patrons of the Games, raising funds and building stadiums. Some, however, have joined the athletes themselves.

Princess Anne of Great Britain, daughter of Queen Elizabeth II, was a member of the British equestrian team in 1976 in Montreal, Canada. She attracted tremendous press coverage, but only after she fell off her horse.

Monaco's Prince Albert did just about as well as Anne when he drove a two-man bobsled at Calgary in 1988. He didn't even come close to the medal class.

But one royal managed to find his way to the winners' platform. In the yachting competition at the 1960 Games in Rome, Italy, Greece's Crown Prince Constantin, who later would become the king, piloted his three-man crew to the gold in the Dragon Class.

Hooray for Hollywood!

For a few of Hollywood's biggest stars, the quickest route to the silver screen was through the Olympics.

First came swimmer Johnny Weissmuller, the 1924 Olympic record-setter in the 400-meter freestyle at Paris and the 1924 and 1928 winner (both in Olympic record time) in the 100-meter freestyle, who went on to star as Tarzan the Ape Man.

Another swimmer, Buster Crabbe, followed Weissmuller into the role of Tarzan. Crabbe and eighteen other athletes tried out for the part just before the 1932 Games at Los Angeles, where he set an Olympic record in the 400-meter freestyle. Later, Crabbe starred in several serials, including Flash Gordon, Buck Rogers, and Billy the Kid.

American Harold Sakata, who took a silver medal in the light-heavyweight weight-lifting competition in 1948 (London), became one of James Bond's archrivals, Oddjob, in *Goldfinger*.

The 1981 Academy Award winner for best picture, *Chariots of Fire,* told the inspiring story of England's Harold Abrahams, the winner of the 100-meter dash at the 1924 Olympics in Paris.

Olympians have been the subjects of other films. For example, superstar Babe Didrikson has been portrayed by actress Susan Clark, 1964 10,000-meter-run champ Billy Mills by actor Robbie Benson, and 1912 hero Jim Thorpe by Burt Lancaster.

Keep an eye open for the stars—and the movies—for the 1992 Games.

Hamill Camel

DOROTHY HAMILL—1976—FIGURE SKATING

At age eight, Dorothy Hamill went skating on a local pond in Riverside, Connecticut, with some neighbors. "They could all skate backwards," she recalled later, "and I couldn't. So I begged my mom to sign me up for skating lessons." Luckily for the sport of skating, her mother agreed.

It took about eight years for Dorothy to move to the top of her sport. In 1973, she won her first of four straight U.S. championships. But as 1976 rolled around, she took aim at the biggest prize of all—the Olympic championship.

She wasn't the favorite at Innsbruck, Austria. Most of the experts had Dorothy pegged for second place, after Dianne deLeeuw of the Netherlands.

Dorothy was ready, however. She had practiced seven hours a day, six days a week, eleven months a year in Denver, Colorado. She had her highly athletic routines, full of double jumps and her famous Hamill Camel—a dizzying spinning move—well polished. And she had her fresh, girl-next-door personality, which came shining through whenever she skated.

From the very start, Dorothy took command. She skated better than she ever had before. By the time she left the ice, she was a national hero in America. Young girls began copying her short wedge haircut and her off-ice trademark eyeglasses. Dorothy starred in ice shows, in commercials, and even in her own television specials. The little girl who couldn't skate backwards had come full circle.

The Soviet Skyscraper

IULIYANA SEMENOVA—1976— BASKETBALL

These days, it seems every great basketball team features a 7-footer. But if the giant is a woman, that's big news.

When the Soviet women's team got to the 1976 Games in Montreal, Canada, a huge 7-foot, 1 3/4-inch woman named Iuliyana Semenova loomed over the rest of the field. And she wasn't just tall—she was strong too.

Few male players have ever enjoyed the size advantage Semenova did. More than a foot taller than her opponents, she took full advantage of her size. She scored 19 points and grabbed 12 rebounds per game as the Soviets cruised to the Olympic title. Four years later in Moscow, she tossed in 21 points and 12.5 rebounds per contest as Russia easily won again, outscoring their rivals by nearly 40 points per game.

The Eagle Landed

MICHAEL EDWARDS—1988— SKI JUMPING

He was the most popular Olympian at the 1988 Winter Games in Calgary, Canada. After all, he was England's best ski jumper. He was also England's *only* ski jumper (the country had no ski-jumping facilities). And he was so lousy, he had the crowd rooting for him . . . to survive!

Michael "The Eagle" Edwards had tried every other bone-crushing sport in the world, usually with bone-crushing results. But nothing could stop him. He stood at the top of the ski-jumping hill, pointed his skis downhill, pushed off, and hoped for the best. His eyesight was weak, his form was lousy, his style worse, and his flights were among the shortest in ski-jumping history. Yet as he laughed, the whole world laughed with him.

He finished last (fortunately not *dead* last) on the 70-meter hill. He was awful. English skiing officials tried to keep him out of the 90-meter event for his safety—and theirs. But they couldn't do it. So The Eagle went right out and finished—what else?—last again.

Tragedy and Triumph

DAN JANSEN—1988—
SPEED SKATING

He was the world speed-skating sprint champion, and America's best hope for the gold. It was his first Olympic race—the 500-meter sprint against Japan's Yasushi Kuroiwa. He crouched behind the starting line, tense.

He jumped the line before the gun went off—false start. He crouched again. This time he got off slowly. Trying to make up the distance he had lost, he took the first turn too quickly. He slammed into the sideboards.

The stands grew quiet. Everyone knew that Dan Jansen had something else on his mind. Seven hours before the race, Dan had been told that his sister Jane was dead.

Dan hadn't wanted to go to the 1988 Winter Games in Calgary, Alberta. He knew that Jane was dying of leukemia. But Jane was a speed skater herself. She urged Dan to go.

Dan lost his first race. But he had another chance—the 1,000 meters.

He got off to a good start. After the first 600 meters, he was nearly one-third of a second ahead of the pack—a big margin in speed skating. Then, with only 200 meters to go, it happened again. Dan hit the ice on the side of his skate. He fell and slid on his hands and knees into the wall. His coach and a teammate helped him to the bench.

Dan cried.

Dan Jansen had suffered. But the fact that he had been on the ice, giving his best at a time of tragedy, won him a special place in Olympic history.

CHAPTER SIX
DARK MOMENTS

The Olympics are a time of triumph and glory, but sometimes scandal, bitter politics, prejudice, and even murder have cast an ugly shadow over the Games.

The First Cancellation

The 1916 Games in Berlin, Germany, promised to be the best Olympics ever. Athletes and fans worldwide were looking forward to these Games with great enthusiasm.

But they never took place. World War I broke out in Europe in 1914, and the Olympics were among its many victims. By the time the war ended in 1918, the entire continent of Europe was ravaged from the fighting.

Many people thought the Olympics were over. And they could have been, if not for the good people of Belgium. The 1920 Games were scheduled for the city of Antwerp, which was heavily battered during the war. Nonetheless, Belgium did the best it could—and it was quite good enough. Despite the interruption of war, the Olympics bounced back better than ever.

The modern Olympics, only twenty-four years old in 1920, had been saved.

The Bungled Relay

The Olympics are supposed to represent brotherhood and unity, but far too often hate and prejudice have entered the picture. One such sad and scandalous moment occured in Berlin, Germany, in 1936.

Dictator Adolf Hitler's government was built on the premise that Jews, blacks, and Latins were inferior to so-called Aryans. Jesse Owens's medal wins enraged Hitler. When he learned that two members of the heavily favored 4 x 100-meter U.S. relay team (Sam Stoller and Marty Glickman) were Jewish, he was beside himself.

Rumors floated around Berlin that the Jewish athletes would not be allowed to compete in the 1936 Olympics. But American coach Lawson Robertson assured the media and everyone else that Stoller and Glickman would run their relay legs.

Behind the scenes, however, the politicians were at work. Pressure began to build. A day before the race, coach Robertson announced that Glickman might be replaced by Jesse Owens. The next day, both Glickman and Stoller learned that they had, in fact, been dropped from the squad.

Had Hitler applied pressure to U.S. team officials to make the change? Robertson denied it. He said that he made the change because he wanted to win. But many suspected that American team leader Avery Brundage had caved in to Hitler's wishes. The American team—Owens,

Ralph Metcalfe, Foy Draper, and Frank Wykoff—
set a new world record (39.8 seconds) to win the
gold. But for Sam Stoller and Marty Glickman,
the only members of the U.S. track team who did
not participate in the '36 Games, the bitter
memory of anti-Semitism would last a lifetime.

When the Pool Turned Red

The world watched with horror in the fall of 1956
as more than 200,000 Soviet soldiers invaded
Hungary to put down an anti-Communist revolt.
Less than a month later, the 1956 Olympics got
under way in Melbourne, Australia. The bitter-
ness of the political struggle spilled over into the
Olympic Games.

Hungary and the Soviet Union met in a
water-polo game. Water polo is generally a rough
sport, but this match was rougher than usual. The
two teams literally slugged it out as Hungary
built a 4-0 lead. The pool turned red from the
blood of players on both sides! Then the violence
spilled into the stands. The crowd of more than
5,500 was almost totally pro-Hungary. The police
were called to restore order. The game was halted,
and the Hungarians were awarded the victory.
They then went on to win the gold.

Though more than thirty-five years have
passed since the day blood flowed at the Olympic
pool, the Soviet Union-Hungary water-polo match
is remembered as a dark moment in the history
of the Games.

Black Power

In 1968, civil rights for blacks was a major issue in the United States. Sprinters Tommie Smith and John Carlos decided to use the Mexico City, Mexico Olympic victory platform to publicize their stand on black civil rights.

In the 200-meter sprint, Smith captured the gold in world-record time (19.83 seconds). Carlos finished third and won the bronze. At the medals ceremony, Smith and Carlos appeared barefoot, each wearing one black glove. As the "Star-Spangled Banner" blared over the public-address system, the two athletes bowed their heads and raised their gloved fists. Among blacks in the United States, this was known as the "black power" salute.

Outrage followed. The International Olympic Committee demanded that the athletes be punished. The U.S. Olympic Committee suspended Smith and Carlos and ordered them to leave Mexico City within forty-eight hours.

Back in the U.S., many people sided with Smith and Carlos. They were exercising their right to free speech and making a statement of support for black athletes. They accused the U.S. Olympic Committee of being racist and caving in to the International Committee.

No matter how you feel about Smith and Carlos's protest, they successfully made their point. It wasn't the last time the Olympic Games would be used for political statements.

Israeli Massacre

Most Olympic drama takes place on the fields, courts, and rinks. But when eight Palestinian terrorists invaded the Israeli athletes' dormitory at the Olympic village in Munich, West Germany, on September 5, 1972, sports were forgotten. An unforgettable day of horror began.

Two Israelis were killed immediately. Another nine were held hostage. The Palestinians warned that they would kill the remaining Israelis unless Israel released 200 political prisoners and the West German government granted the terrorists safe passage out of Germany.

Television cameras focused on the dormitory. Viewers around the world watched in horror as the armed terrorists patrolled the balcony.

Late that evening, hope arose that the hostages would be saved. The terrorists accepted an offer to leave Germany. They were transported to the airport, still holding the hostages. There, expert German riflemen ambushed the Palestinians and shot three of the terrorists. But in the battle, two other terrorists, one German policeman, and all of the Israeli athletes were killed. Americans watched as TV broadcaster Jim McKay said, in tears, "They're all gone!"

In mourning, the Olympics came to a standstill. All events for September 6 were suspended. When the International Olympic Committee president, Avery Brundage, announced that the Games would continue, many athletes, coaches, and fans refused to compete. Two decades later, the massacre of the Israelis remains the blackest day in Olympic history.

The Late Show

Sprinters live by the clock, usually in hundredths of seconds. But a standard watch, showing hours and minutes only, and an old schedule proved the downfall of American sprinters Rey Robinson and Eddie Hart at the 1972 Olympics, in Munich, West Germany, and caused a moment of bitter debate.

Hart and Robinson were both expected to go for the gold in the 100-meter dash. Both had qualified for the quarterfinals, which they thought were scheduled for 7:00 p.m. Unfortunately, the schedule their coach, Stan Wright, was working with was more than a year old.

As they stood in the ABC-TV video truck at around 4:00 p.m., the two noticed on the monitor a heat of the 100 meters ready to get under way. "It's probably just a replay of an earlier race," they said. But it wasn't. Their races were ready to roll and they were miles away.

An ABC vehicle rushed the pair to the stadium, but it was too late. A protest failed and the two sprinters were eliminated.

Hart and Robinson were bitter. "I trained ten years for this moment and now it's all gone," said a tearful Hart.

Tip-off

Fencing is usually seen as a classy gentlemen's game. But in 1976 there was a genuine fencing scandal. Judging the ancient sport of fencing used to be one of the toughest jobs at the Olympics. Fencers must touch their opponent's body with the tip of their swords. And depending upon which sword is being used—the sabre, foil, or epee—the touch must come within certain parts of the rival's uniform. Touches came so fast that judges' naked eyes often missed them. The development of the electronic tip, which produced a special signal when it made contact with a fencer's uniform, revolutionized the sport and helped make judging easier.

Just when fencing had taken this high-tech step into the twenty-first century, Soviet Boris Onischenko got into the act. Boris was so desperate to win that he resorted to cheating. At the 1976 Montreal Games, the Soviet teacher and former world pentathlon champion rigged his electronic epee so that it would record touches that never happened.

But Onischenko didn't get the last laugh— or any laugh at all! His opponents were very confused. Boris's electronic tip was recording touches that the other fencers never felt. An investigation followed, and his trick was discovered.

Boris was instantly disqualified and shipped home. The last anyone heard, the former teacher and champion fencer was driving a taxi.

Boycott I

When Soviet troops invaded Afghanistan in December 1979 to keep anti-Communist rebels under control, the world was outraged.

In Washington, President Jimmy Carter was in trouble—and he knew it. American hostages were being held captive by government forces in Iran. And now the Russians were overrunning the Afghans. How could he express his displeasure?

The 1980 Summer Olympics were scheduled for Moscow. In an attempt to punish the Russians and demonstrate his own strength as a leader, Carter ordered the U.S. Olympic team to boycott the Games. "How can we send our fine young men and women to compete in the Soviet Union at a time like this?" said the president. And so the Americans stayed home.

American opinions ranged from total support for the Carter boycott to total opposition. Athletes who had worked for a decade or more preparing for their Olympic opportunity were disappointed. Some spoke out strongly against the president. Meanwhile, Carter begged other nations to stay at home as well. Many did, though others, like England and Australia, left the decision to individual athletes.

Once again politics had played a major role in the Olympic Games.

Boycott II

You could almost bet on it. When the U.S. led a boycott of the 1980 Olympics in the Soviet Union, you knew what the Soviets would do when the 1984 Olympics came to the United States.

For several years, the Soviets promised that they'd forget how the Americans had spoiled their Games in 1980. But when the final day came to sign up for the '84 Games, the Soviets said no. "America had no business in the Vietnam War," they cried. "The Americans illegally invaded Granada, too." The Soviets cited every possible American "violation." The end result—the Soviets and many of their allies stayed home.

Johnson's Downfall

As Canada's Ben Johnson stood atop the victory platform in Seoul, South Korea, in 1988, his world seemed perfect. He had shattered the world record in the 100-meter dash (9.79 seconds) and beaten his archrival, Carl Lewis of the U.S. And now, with the bright sun reflecting off his brand-new gold medal and the band playing "Oh Canada" in the background, all was well.

Not for long. Within twenty-four hours, the news was out. Ben Johnson had tested positive for steroids, drugs which are designed to add muscle and body bulk. Steroids are illegal according to

Olympic rules. Johnson was forced to leave Seoul in disgrace. His record was wiped out. His gold medal went to Carl Lewis. He was suspended from track for two years and told he could never again compete for Canada. The ban was lifted in 1991.

Drugs had turned a glorious moment of victory into disappointment and disgrace.

Boxing's Blackest Day

It was clear that the 1988 bantamweight fight in Seoul between Alexander Hristov of Bulgaria and Byun Jong Il of the home team, South Korea, was going Hristov's way. The referee, a man from New Zealand named Keith Walker, had penalized Byun a point in each of the first two rounds for leading with his head. The crowd, composed largely of Koreans, was unhappy. Some Koreans decided to take matters into their own hands, and the day turned ugly.

When the decision was announced (Hristov won 4-1), a riot broke out. Lee Heung Soo, the Korean team trainer, vaulted the ropes and entered the ring. He went after referee Walker. Others quickly followed, including several Korean security guards, who first ripped off their "official" yellow jackets. Other spectators attacked the judges at ringside, destroying the official match scoresheet.

Some of the other referees, waiting to work other bouts, ran into the ring to help Walker.

Eventually, they were able to rescue him. But on his way to the dressing room, Walker was attacked by still another security guard, who tried to kick him in the head.

Walker had had enough. He gathered his clothes and immediately left for the airport. He wanted to leave South Korea—fast.

Meanwhile, the beaten Byun protested the decision by sitting in the middle of the ring for over an hour.

Korean Olympic leaders were disgusted. "We've worked hard for seven years to make these the best Olympics ever," said one. "And in just a few moments, some of our own people have destroyed that dream. We are ashamed."

CHAPTER SEVEN
AMAZING UPSETS

Never! Impossible! He can't win. That team has no chance. Right? Wrong! In the Olympics anything can happen.

The Barefoot Hero

Abebe Bikila—practically no one had ever heard that name before the 1960 Olympics in Rome, Italy. Ethiopia's Bikila was buried deep in the pack at the marathon starting line. And that's where everyone figured he would finish.

Surprise! Running barefoot, Abebe moved right to the front at the start, staying with the leaders for most of the first half of the race. Then he took over the lead. By the time he reached the stadium, he was the talk of the town. His time of 2:15:16.2 set an Olympic—and world—record! What an upset! He was the first Ethiopian to win an Olympic medal. Later, Bikila admitted that it was only the third marathon of his life.

But it wasn't his last. Four years later, Abebe moved to the starting line in Tokyo, Japan. This time everyone knew his name. But his chances of winning a second marathon were very slim.

Only forty days before the race, he had an operation in which his appendix was removed. No one thought he could ever get ready for the grueling 26.2-mile marathon. No athlete, not even a healthy one, had ever won a second Olympic marathon crown.

But Abebe Bikila still had surprises in store. He won the gold and set *another* world record.

Abebe's luck ran out when he tried for a third straight gold medal in Mexico City, Mexico, in 1968. Injuries destroyed any chance he had; he dropped out after only 10 miles. A year later, an auto accident paralyzed his lower body and forced him into a wheelchair. Though he began competing in wheelchair sports, Bikila died a few years later at age forty-one. But he will always be remembered for his amazing upset victories.

Is It Over?

From the first time Olympic referees tossed a basketball in the air in 1936, the U.S. owned the sport. Over the next thirty-six years, American teams won sixty-two straight games. Proud U.S. fans claimed that their country could put together a dozen teams that could win the Olympics.

The U.S. was the clear-cut favorite at the 1972 Games in Munich, West Germany. After breezing through the early rounds, the U.S. team met the Soviet team. And the Soviets were good! In fact, the Soviets led by 8 points with only five minutes to go!

American fans were shocked. Then a pair of Doug Collins free throws gave America a 50-49 lead with just three seconds to play.

That's when things got strange.

The Soviets inbounded the ball and two of the remaining seconds clicked off the clock. But the Brazilian referee noticed a commotion at the scorer's table. The Soviets claimed they had tried to call a time-out after the first Collins free-throw. The time-out was awarded and the timer left one second on the clock. Then R. William Jones of Great Britain, the head of the International Amateur Basketball Federation, stepped in. Although he didn't have the authority to do so, he ordered *three* seconds put back on the clock. In fact, *two* seconds were added to the clock.

Given another chance, the Soviets threw a length-of-the-court pass to Sasha Belov, who pushed past two American defenders to score at the buzzer. The Soviets had won an incredible upset victory.

Maybe. United States coaches filed an immediate protest. Through the night, the protest committee met, hearing from coaches and watching videotape. Thirteen hours later, the committee voted, 3-2, to deny the American protest. The Russian victory was secure.

As the runner-up team, the American players won silver medals. They refused to accept them and did not appear at the medal ceremony. Somewhere, the 1972 basketball silver medals rest in a bank vault. And twenty years later, people are still talking about this incredible game.

The Unknown Soldier

Although the sportswriters scrambled to learn every detail about the lives of virtually every Olympic athlete at the 1964 Tokyo Games, no one bothered with American distance runner Billy Mills. No American had ever won the Olympic 10,000-meter title. Only one had ever finished as high as second, and world-record holder Ron Clarke of Australia was considered a sure thing in Japan. Forget Mills, they reasoned. He hasn't got a chance.

At the start, Clarke, as advertised, grabbed an early lead. By the midway point, he had put away most of the competition. But Mohamed Gammoudi of Tunisia and the surprising Billy Mills were still on his tail with one lap to go.

Mills finally pulled even with the Australian and the two raced on. In an attempt to pass slower runners (who were a lap behind), Clarke shoved Mills out of the way. When he turned to apologize, Gammoudi sneaked past both of them and took the lead.

In the backstretch, Clarke and Gammoudi raced stride for stride. Then, with only about 100 yards to go, Mills kicked into high gear, sprinted past his rivals, and went on to win in 28:24.4—a new Olympic record.

It was one of the most shocking upsets in Olympic history. Mills's story was told around the world. (In fact, Robbie Benson starred as the gold-medal champ in the *Billy Mills Story* in the movies.) It was an inspiring tale. Orphaned at age twelve, Mills was a full-blooded Sioux who went on to the University of Kansas, then became a Marine officer. And his Olympic time of 28:24.4? It was the fastest Mills had ever run the 10,000 meters—by *more than 46 seconds!*

Miracle on Ice

Since the mid-1950s, the Soviet Union has always seemed to have the best ice hockey team in the world. Everyone agreed they would win the gold medal at Lake Placid in 1980.

The U.S., on the other hand, looked positively hopeless. Supertough coach Herb Brooks had prepared his pickup team of young college players the best he could. But when they played against the Soviets in a pre-Olympic game, they lost 10-3. It was clear the U.S. team and the Soviet team didn't belong on the same ice.

But somebody forgot to tell Brooks's players. Playing in a tough division that featured top teams from Czechoslovakia and Sweden, the Americans weren't even expected to make the medal round. Only two teams from each of the two divisions would go that far.

In the opener, Sweden scored the first goal and led 2-1 with less than a minute to play. That's when Brooks pulled his goaltender to get an extra skater on the ice. It's a gamble that rarely works. More often, the opponents wind up scoring a goal. But this time it was the perfect move. With twenty-seven seconds to go, Bill Baker scored for the U.S. and the game ended in a tie.

Next came the high-flying Czechs. They too scored the first goal. But the U.S. rallied to tie at 2-2 after one period and went on to shock their opponents, 7-3. The Americans had met their top two challengers and had not lost. Things were beginning to get interesting.

Against Norway, the U.S. again gave up the first goal and then won easily, 5-1. It was no contest against Romania, with the Americans winning 7-2. Against West Germany, the U.S. gave up the first *two* goals and then closed to win 4-2.

Shockingly, the Americans moved on to the medal round. But the Soviets stood right in their path. The world champs!

It was no surprise that the Soviets scored first. But then Buzz Schneider tied the game for the U.S. Russian Sergei Makarov made it 2-1, but with only one second to go in the opening period, Mark Johnson knotted it up again.

Did the U.S. youngsters have a shot? Perhaps. Strangely, the Soviet coach switched goaltenders as the second period opened, replacing superstar Vladislav Tretiak with backup Vladimir Myshkin. But the substitute held the U.S. scoreless while Aleksandr Maltsev gave the Soviets a 3-2 lead.

Between periods two and three, quiet confidence began building in the U.S. locker room. No one thought this team had any business playing in the same arena as the Soviets. But here they were, only one goal behind, with twenty minutes left to play. For this young American team, there was real hope.

At 8:39 in the third period, Mark Johnson picked up a loose puck and banged it past goalie Myshkin. Tie! The roof seemed as if it were about to come off the arena. Little more than a minute later, U.S. captain Mike Eruzione fired a 30-foot screen shot into the Soviet net and the U.S. led, 4-3. The miracle was beginning to happen.

For the final ten minutes, the Soviets fired barrage after barrage at U.S. goaltender Jim Craig. He stopped them all. As the clock wound down, ABC-TV's Al Michaels uttered those now famous words, "Do you believe in miracles? Yes!"

When it was all over, players cried, fans cried, even tough Herb Brooks had to hide from the press until he was back in control.

Still, there was one more challenge: Finland. A U.S. loss would doom the Americans to third place and give the Soviets the title. To the young U.S. team, this was unthinkable!

For the sixth time in seven games, the opponents scored first. And after two periods, Finland had a 2-1 lead. But these Americans had come too far to blow it now. First, Dave Christian fed Phil Verchota, who scored on a 15-foot slapshot. It was 2-2. Rob McClanahan stuffed in the go-ahead goal three and a half minutes later. Finally Mark Johnson added an insurance goal with three and a half minutes to go.

They won the gold! Now *everyone* believed in miracles!

The First Miracle

The "Miracle on Ice" at Lake Placid in 1980 was not the first U.S. hockey miracle.

In the 1960 Games at Squaw Valley, California, the American team had only two chances to win gold on the ice: slim and none. An opening-round come-from-behind victory over Czechoslovakia got the American team fired up. Victories over Australia, Sweden, and Germany followed quickly.

American hockey fans began to get excited. But the wiser heads urged caution. The red-hot Canadian team was next.

No sweat. Sparked by a second-period goal by Paul Johnson, whose son later played for the 1980 team, the Americans pulled off a remarkable 2-1 upset.

Next came the Soviets, a team the U.S. had never beaten. The Soviets held a 2-1 lead through the opening period. But the Christian brothers, Billy and Roger, combined for goals late in the second period and again with five minutes to go in the game. With a 3-2 lead, U.S. goaltender Jack McCartan withstood a heavy Soviet attack to sew up the amazing victory.

Now only Czechoslovakia stood between the Americans and their miracle gold medal. The U.S. had won their earlier match-up, but the American players were exhausted from their hard-fought victory over the Soviets. The Czechs scored just eight seconds into the game and held a 4-3 edge after two periods.

Then a strange thing happened. During the break between periods, the captain of the Soviet team, Nikolai Sologubov, visited the American locker room. Having lost to the U.S. team, Sologubov wanted his conquerors to go all the way. Using sign language (he spoke no English), he suggested that the players pep themselves up by breathing some pure oxygen. It was a brilliant idea. Feeling fresh, the Americans reeled off six straight goals in the final period and won easily, 9-4. The miracle of Squaw Valley was in the history books.

CHAPTER EIGHT

THE OLYMPICS TODAY AND TOMORROW

Every Olympiad brings changes and surprises. What will happen at Albertville and Barcelona? Stay tuned.

South Africa Returns

When the 1992 Summer Olympics get under way in Barcelona, Spain, South Africa will be there—for the first time in thirty-two years.

After the 1960 Olympics, many of the world's nations protested against South Africa's racist policy of apartheid. Until recently, whites and blacks were completely separate in South Africa, and laws denied blacks human rights.

As a result, South Africa was banned from all international games. In fact, in 1976 at Montreal, Canada, African nations demanded that New Zealand be barred. Why? Because a New Zealand rugby team had played some games in South Africa. Since rugby isn't an Olympic sport, the International Olympic Committee said that it couldn't do anything about it. Still, several African nations plus Iraq and Guyana pulled out of the Montreal Games.

Now, in the '90s, South Africa's racial policies have changed. The nation has been welcomed back to the sports world and to the 1992 Olympics.

The Games Divide

Today the Olympics mean huge crowds, athletes from hundreds of nations, and weeks of competition. But when the modern Olympics first began in 1896, only 311 athletes, all men, showed up in Athens. They represented only thirteen countries. No more than twenty-nine countries ever appeared until forty-four competed in Paris in 1924.

Eventually, the numbers began to grow and grow. By 1988 in Seoul, South Korea, 160 countries and more than 9,600 athletes saw action. The Winter Games grew too.

Recently it became evident that it was too difficult to stage both Winter and Summer Games in the same year. So 1992 will mark the last time the two Olympics will be held together. In 1994, the Winter Games start a new schedule. The next Winter Games will be in 1998, then 2002, 2006, etc. The Summer Games will continue the standard schedule, meeting in Atlanta, Georgia, in 1996 and continuing in 2000, 2004, 2008, and so on.

The Pro Game

When the U.S. lost its first men's Olympic basketball game in 1972, Americans began to grumble. "Why are we playing with a pickup team of college players when the rest of the world uses full-time teams and experienced talent? Our best players are professionals; why can't they play?"

The Americans bounced back to win the basketball gold at Montreal, Canada, in 1976 and, after the 1980 boycott, at Los Angeles, California, in 1984. But a third-place finish, behind Russia and Yugoslavia in 1988 sounded an alarm. Within months, Olympic basketball rules were changed. From now on, professionals (spelled NBA in the U.S.A.) will be part of Olympic hoops action.

When the world's best get together at Barcelona, Spain, in 1992, at least three quarters of the U.S. team plus coach Chuck Daly will be chosen straight out of the National Basketball Association. Americans are confident that the likes of Magic Johnson, Patrick Ewing, and David Robinson will be just what the hoops doctor ordered.

One Germany Again—But U.S.S.R. Divides

At the end of World War II, Germany was divided into two countries: East and West Germany. However, the two nations continued to send one combined team to the Olympics—until 1968. Then what once had been a single powerful German team became two powerful German teams, East Germany and West Germany.

But when the Berlin Wall fell on November 9, 1989, the world sports scene changed too. With the two Germanys now one, the two German Olympic teams were reunited too. The 1992 Games at Albertville, France, will mark the return of the single German squad. Anticipating the merger, coaches from the rest of the world are not sleeping well.

But whereas Germany will become a single Olympic force, the very powerful Soviet Union team is now dissolving into several smaller teams. In 1991, many of the Baltic states declared their independence from the Soviet Union. Three of these states—Estonia, Latvia, and Lithuania—have been given consent by the International Olympic Committee to field separate teams for the 1992 Games, and more may follow. This break-up may have a significant effect on the Soviet Union's medal-winning ways.

THE OLYMPIC GAMES

			COMPETITORS		NATIONS
WINTER			Men	Women	Represented
I	1924	CHAMONIX, FRANCE	281	13	16
II	1928	ST. MORITZ, SWITZERLAND	468	27	25
III	1932	LAKE PLACID, U.S.A.	274	32	17
IV	1936	GARMISCH-PARTENKIRCHEN, GERMANY	675	80	28
—	1940	cancelled because of war	—	—	—
—	1944	cancelled because of war	—	—	—
V	1948	ST. MORITZ, SWITZERLAND	636	77	28
VI	1952	OSLO, NORWAY	623	109	30
VII	1956	CORTINA D'AMPEZZO, ITALY	686	132	32
VIII	1960	SQUAW VALLEY, U.S.A.	521	144	30
IX	1964	INNSBRUCK, AUSTRIA	986	200	36

	Year	City	Men	Women	Represented
X	1968	GRENOBLE, FRANCE	1081	212	37
XI	1972	SAPPORO, JAPAN	1015	217	35
XII	1976	INNSBRUCK, AUSTRIA	900	228	37
XIII	1980	LAKE PLACID, U.S.A.	833	234	37
XIV	1984	SAREJEVO, YUGOSLAVIA	1002	276	49
XV	1988	CALGARY, CANADA	1128	317	57
XVI	1992	ALBERTVILLE, FRANCE			
XVII	1994	LILLEHAMMER, NORWAY			

SUMMER

	Year	City	Men	Women	Represented
I	1896	ATHENS, GREECE	311	0	13
II	1900	PARIS, FRANCE	1319	11	22
III	1904	ST. LOUIS, U.S.A.	681	6	12
—	1906	ATHENS, GREECE	877	7	20
IV	1908	LONDON, GREAT BRITAIN	1999	36	23
V	1912	STOCKHOLM, SWEDEN	2490	57	28
VI	1916	cancelled because of war	—	—	—
VII	1920	ANTWERP, BELGIUM	2543	64	29
VIII	1924	PARIS, FRANCE	2956	136	44
IX	1928	AMSTERDAM, HOLLAND	2724	290	46
X	1932	LOS ANGELES, U.S.A.	1281	127	37

SUMMER

			Men	Women	Represented
XI	1936	BERLIN, GERMANY	3738	328	49
XII	1940	cancelled because of war	—	—	—
XIII	1944	cancelled because of war	—	—	—
XIV	1948	LONDON, GREAT BRITAIN	3714	385	59
XV	1952	HELSINKI, FINLAND	4407	518	69
XVI	1956	MELBOURNE, AUSTRALIA	2958	384	67
XVII	1960	ROME, ITALY	4738	610	83
XVIII	1964	TOKYO, JAPAN	4457	683	93
XIX	1968	MEXICO CITY, MEXICO	4750	781	112
XX	1972	MUNICH, WEST GERMANY	5848	1299	122
XXI	1976	MONTREAL, CANADA	4834	1251	92
XXII	1980	MOSCOW, U.S.S.R.	4265	1088	81
XXIII	1984	LOS ANGELES, U.S.A.	5458	1620	141
XXIV	1988	SEOUL, SOUTH KOREA	7105	2476	160
XXV	1992	BARCELONA, SPAIN			
XXVI	1996	ATLANTA, U.S.A.			